A Child Development
Point of View

A Child Development Point of View

James L. Hymes, Jr.

Professor of Elementary Education
George Peabody College for Teachers

GREENWOOD PRESS, PUBLISHERS
WESTPORT, CONNECTICUT

Library of Congress Cataloging in Publication Data

Hymes, James L   1913-
    A child development point of view.

    Reprint of the ed. published by Prentice-Hall, Engle-
wood Cliffs, N. J.
    1. Child development. I. Title.
[LB1115.H95   1977]   370.15'8   77-8989
ISBN 0-8371-9723-6

Originally published in 1955 by Prentice-Hall, Inc.,
Englewood Cliffs, N.J.

Reprinted with the permission of Prentice-Hall, Inc.

Reprinted in 1977 by Greenwood Press, Inc.

Library of Congress catalog card number 77-8989

ISBN 0-8371-9723-6

Printed in the United States of America

Preface

 $\mathcal{T}$he stresses and strains in today's living have stirred a wide interest in mental health. In particular, the call everywhere is for preventive efforts—those which build strength into people.

Many persons profess to work in this key area of prevention. Too much that goes on under this good name, however, concentrates on the early diagnosis and treatment of difficulties. Important as this work is, the focus is still on ill health. The preventive task is left undone.

In contrast, good classroom teachers rarely call their work "mental health," preventive or otherwise. Yet, more than they know, good teachers are hard at work building strength. In faculty meetings, workshops, in-service, and college courses teachers are studying children. In their classrooms they are acting on their knowledge to build good feelings into children. This is health. This is prevention. This is the goal *A Child Development Point of View* aims to further.

JAMES L. HYMES, JR.

Table of Contents

"What! Let Them Get Away with Murder?"
41. "But Some Ages Are Anti-Adult," 44.

The Child Development Background, 48.
Toward the "Real McCoy," 49. Not Anything Goes, 51. A Strong Chain, 54. The
Time Will Come, 56. Slowly, Gradually, 58.
The Time Is Always Now, 61. Some Special
Social Conditions, 63. At Sixes and Sevens,
66. A Saving Grace, 70. You, in Your
Classroom, 75. Rough Estimates of Growth,
75. Listen! 78. Everlastingly on the Go,
81. "Child" Has a Capital "I" in the Middle, 84. Some More Specific Suggestions,
87. Discussion Time, 89. "Whatever They
Want to Do Is O. K.," 90. "You Can Do It
in Sports, but . . . ," 92. "But with 35 in
a Class!" 95. "You Will Make Them Soft,"
96.

The Child Development Background, 102.
Some Special Social Conditions, 108. A
"Reducing Diet," 110. School: A Work-
shop, 112. You, in Your Classroom, 115.
Flowing from Your Feelings, 117. The Big-
ness of Life, 120. Facts, Skills, and Know-
How, 123. The People's Choice, 124. Some

1

You Are a Teacher

You are a teacher. Let's assume that you have thirty-five youngsters in your class. And we can take for granted one more thing: You want to do a good job. You want your youngsters to learn and you want them to like learning.

If this is you, Child Development can help you do what you want to do. It makes no difference what age your youngsters are. If you are lucky enough to have fewer than thirty-five children, that certainly will help. But young children or teen-agers, nursery school or high school, twenty in the group

1

or forty, Child Development has some generalizations about your students—ideas you can use.

Ever since the mid-1920's Child Development has
been an over-all name, shorthand for good things for
children. But it has been more than that. It has also
been a distinct field of study. Like mathematics, history, astronomy. You could major in it, minor in it,
get a master's degree in it, a doctorate.

Child Development, the field of study, has three
big concerns: It looks at normal children, at well
children, at the run of youngsters just as they feed
out of homes into schools, churches, camps, onto the
play lots and the streets. It looks at what they typically do—at what they do just because they are
children.

It looks at normal children and at well children
of all ages—from the very start of a life in the pre-
natal period, into infancy, into the preschool years,
when boys and girls are in school, into adolescence
and even beyond.

And Child Development is concerned with the
whole child:

Whole . . . up and down, from his very start to
his present and with at least a peek into his future.

Whole . . . across a child's middle and back
again: a head, a heart, a body, a soul; his intellec-

tual, his social, his physical, emotional, and spiritual growth.

Whole . . . the school child, the home child, the youngster in his club; the child with brothers and sisters and friends; with his parents and his teacher and neighbors; everywhere a youngster is in a day and with everyone he meets.

Whole . . . as an individual, but also as a human tied in to the total broad circle of all people—this child, boy or girl, ten-year-old or sixteen or six, as a person, acting in many ways as all other people do act and have to act.

As a field of study Child Development borrows a little from psychology, a little from psychiatry, a little from sociology. It takes some ideas from pediatrics, and some from nutrition. Anthropology chips in some of its findings. A great many disciplines—group work, religious education, industrial relations—all give something to Child Development.

This field is eclectic. That is a nice way of saying: Child Development steals from other disciplines what it can use. But it does not steal everything. It is very selective, a kind of gentleman thief. It takes only ideas which can throw light on normal development, on total development, although it takes them wherever it can find them.

Look at your class. Your school doors are open to everyone. You have a cross-section of your whole community, a huge handful of whatever age your group is. These are the people—well children, typical youngsters just as they come along—that Child Development has been studying and trying better to understand.

Now look at your group again. You see more than brains at work. In the course of a day your youngsters are playing, moving, talking, listening and looking, eating, "toilet-ing," feeling shy and feeling "fight-y." In the time you have them, a child's total life goes on. Child Development has been studying that totality, trying better to comprehend how the parts fit together.

Child Development is still a new field. Already, though, it has uncovered some things that help people, and it has spotted some that hurt. It has developed generalizations that seem to be true about man just because he is Man. Not because he is poor, orphaned, blind, neglected, slower-thinking, fatter-than-average, or because he has a sore throat. They are generalizations about the broad sweep of boys and girls, typical youngsters: one head, two arms and two legs, able to talk and think, and with all the other characteristics that make us men and not mice.

These generalizations can strengthen your sensitivity. They can sharpen your goals so that you know what is apt to count most, as you teach boys and girls. They can bring you more in tune with your young people.

Maybe you teach in a slum or a fancy suburb. Maybe you are off in the country or plunk in the middle of a big city. You may work in an elementary school, or as a separate subject-matter teacher in a high school, or maybe you go from grade to grade as a special teacher. No matter what your situation: You teach boys and girls . . . they are human . . . and Child Development has some ideas about people like that.

2

Your Youngsters Must Like You

*T*he first statement Child
Development can make about children is a very
direct one. It comes to you straight from the shoulder: *Your youngsters have to think you are a
"honey."* Tops! A "peach"! They cannot think of
you simply as "Teacher" or as one more adult with
whom they are stuck. They cannot have a lukewarm
feeling or a passive "She's O.K. . . . I guess." If
you want to get the best work out of boys and girls,
if you want good discipline, if you want the best for
them, they must think that you are something
special.

6

The Child Development Background

This fact—your children must like you—comes first because its roots go down deep, to the very beginning of life. An infant seeks above all the comforting sense that the adults around him are good people—kindly, warm, approving.

A baby has to feel this way. He is a helpless creature. At first he cannot lift his head. He cannot turn over. He cannot use his hands. He cannot move. If he is hungry he hurts inside, and he goes on hurting until adults do something. If he is uncomfortable he is sore, and he stays sore until adults do something. If he is lonely he is wretched, and he stays wretched until adults do something.

The young child counts on all the big people around him for food, for changing diapers, for baths, for lifting him and moving him. That you know, but you may not know that the baby reads a meaning into all these simple deeds. If they are done gently, quickly, gladly, they spell out "Love" to the child. The world is saying "Welcome" and that is the one word an infant needs to hear.

Some Child Development people sum up this central need of the start of life by the term "A Sense of

Trust." When a child discovers it you can see the shine all over him. He learns that the people around him are decent, they are interested, they are kind and gentle. (The adults are good people. That means he must be a pretty good fellow, too.)

The baby who feels this way is off to a good start. He is happy and cheerful, not fretting or screwed up and tense. He will grow. He can relax. He won't have a little knot of worries tightening up his insides. He can blossom out into the best he can become.

An infant is thrown to the wolves if he does not get this welcome feeling. But little children are not the only ones. You would not expect something so fundamental to be washed off the slate just because a child gets older. It is not. Never is there a time when this feeling does not count.

You know this to be true from your own living. All of us, as adults, are at our best when we like the people around us. We are not the helpless, dependent creatures that babies are, but the need to like and to be liked is never far below the surface, even at our advanced ages.)

Put adults in any new situation: a job, a camp, a college, any place. One of the very first things we have to determine is: What is *he* like? He—the boss, the principal, the supervisor. Is he friendly?

Will he like me? Can I count on that solid satisfying comfortable Sense of Trust, or must I put some of my energies into watching *him,* keeping an eye out, being on my guard?

With people we like we open up. We talk. We can be clever. We do our best thinking. Others tighten us up or they shut us up, or their impact makes us argue more and disagree. Our friends let us be ourselves, our best selves. We do justice to all our abilities. We don't stammer or forget or become blocked and angry.

Sound scientific evidence backs up this observation that even adults do their best work when they like and trust the humans around them. Studies show that when workers feel their factory to be a friendly place, they produce. When their job is just a job—nobody knows their names, nobody cares—not as much work gets done.

Studies on members of our armed forces indicate the same thing. When fighting men feel they are on a team—their leaders are concerned about them as individuals, the men like their leaders—morale is high. The men stand and fight; they take what comes along; they do their level best.

Other evidence shows that the same force operates with school-age youngsters. Put a friendly leader with a group: he smiles easily, can tell a joke and take one, he cares about the boys. The youngsters become better children. They work harder, they get along better with each other. Give the same children a colder, less responsive leader. The work is done less eagerly, the children have less bounce, they are more at each other's throats.

We start life compelled by our very helplessness to rely on the goodwill of stronger adults. But humans are social. We are close to people all our days. We need people, and we rely on people. Our whole human nature pulls us toward people. We cannot live completely alone and like it. No matter how far from infancy we are we have to be with humans we can like. Failing that, we are dragged down with worry, with anxiety, with fear.

"I Like You . . . I Want to Be Like You"

From the very beginning friendly humans play a second important role in children's lives. They lift youngsters up by being an ideal.

The little child must rely on his parents. Mother and father do good things for him. They feed him, they clean him, they clothe him and comfort him. He gets his parents' love. But the child does something in return: He *gives* his good behavior. Because humans are kind to him and gentle, he becomes a human. This is the bargain he makes, unknown to himself and never spelled out. He likes adults, and then he pays them the compliment of growing to be like them.

A child—baby, school-age, adolescent—has to learn many things in order to fit into our society. No one could ever teach him everything. No one can even remember all the little specifics that go into making a civilized person. We can name the big things: don't kill and don't steal . . wear clothes and talk our language . . . use a knife and fork and spoon. . . . But much more is incorporated into each child as he becomes a member of the human family.

No one teaches it, not in words or in specific instruction. Yet all of us teach it all the time. We teach through how we stand, through what we say, through what we do. Our behavior, minute after minute and day after day, teaches; and the child learns.

He learns *if* he wants to be one of us. Then he sees the lessons. Then he remembers them. Then they become a part of him. But note the one essential condition: The child must feel that we are good, he must be "sold" on us. Then he has a reason for paying attention, and a reason for making the effort.

Let this attitude on the child's part be missing— then the task of civilizing children becomes insuperable. You have to tell them so much. You have to remind over and over. You have to instruct so often. And your words tend to fall on barren soil. You say the right thing, but no one hears it. You say good words, but they ricochet.

This is the trouble with delinquent children. Many of them have really cared for no one. No one has cared for them. People have punished them. Talked at them. People have yelled, and people have nagged. The delinquent's life has been full of verbal tellings, but his life has also been empty of love. These children have had no model, no ideal, no one whose love rewarded them when they made an effort.

We are not talking about an adolescent who posts a photo of some movie star on the wall and copies her hair-do and her pose. The need to love is an unconscious process. Children post photos in their hearts. They have pictures in their minds of good parents, of good teachers. These are the pictures they copy—*their* goals, *their* attitudes, *their* whole way of life. Without such images no one way of acting is much better than any other.

Wanting your children to like you then is not some simple, unimportant, extracurricular activity. You cannot be casual about it, working at it if and when you have time. It is the basis of everything you do. Succeed in it and your children will work. Succeed in it and you will, slowly but surely, get your youngsters' best behavior.

School Is a Testing Ground

The school-going child is not very far from infancy, even the big strapping brute in twelfth grade. He sounds independent. He wants to be independent. Compared to the few little tricks a baby can do on his own, the high-schooler is a master magician. But even this older age needs desperately to like the adults who teach him.

The elementary school child, particularly youngsters in the primary grades, are closer to babyhood. The search for trust—the sureness that people are good—is a keener search for them. It gurgles up to the top of their concerns more easily, more quickly. Each new situation sets off the trigger. This need which in babyhood was all-important can still, at the slightest jiggle, be very compelling, very pervasive.

But, five-year-old or fifteen-year-old, school children have tested their parents. School is their second big chance. They have made some discoveries with the first team on the schedule, their mothers and fathers. Now they are facing the second team to come along—teachers. They have to see if the same answers hold true.

Ideally—through being loved at home, cuddled and enjoyed, fed, allowed to grow, encouraged to play and to have ideas—youngsters come into school with a beginning conviction: People are fine . . . This is a good world in which to be a child . . . I guess I'm O.K., too.

But some children will enter school unsure. From harshness and coldness, from being kept small or overprotected, from nagging or neglect, they won't feel trustful of people. They won't feel content about themselves. They will be tense and worried, with a gnawing anxiety inside.

School is new; things may be different here. Teachers are new; these adults may act differently. The children in the group are new. And the child himself is new: losing teeth, getting taller, more coordinated, a better talker, more able to concentrate. He is his old self (he cannot slough off his yesteryears, good or bad), but he is a new person, too. Each day, each year, is something of a new start—another chance to discover new answers to an old, old question.

This is a child's life. Even when his parents have been and are being wonderful to him, he cannot rest on his laurels. His growth pushes him out into new fields. If he stops he is lost. His parents must be good people, but his teachers must also be good people, and his neighbors, his community, his world. The child's own development makes him need to find new answers constantly, and good answers continuously.

Some Children Are Magnets

Some children have no trouble liking all the adults around them. The reason is simple: All the adults like them! These lucky youngsters have winning ways that warm every person they come near. Perhaps their bright eyes do the trick. Or their flaxen hair. Or these youngsters may have a knack of reminding everyone of a cocker spaniel puppy.

Alert boys and girls often have this effect. Polite children sometimes collect love with no effort at all. Clean children do it. Sometimes a child has appeal just because he was smart enough to pick the right parents: prominent parents, powerful parents, well-established folk, or wealthy.

You have thirty-five children in your class. A handful will have some magnetic quality. They will draw out your smiles and friendly glances and approval . . . and they in turn will think you are the salt of the earth. But all your children have to feel this way, not simply a lucky, favored few.

You give your youngsters an intelligence test or an achievement test. Some boys and girls will score very high. Maybe these are "the daring young men on the flying trapeze."

Listen to your group. Some chatter away, full of bright remarks. Some are always in the lead and know exactly what to do. "They fly through the air with the greatest of ease."

Look at your class in the lunchroom or on the playground. Some have flair and some are so nimble. "Their motions are graceful, the girls they do please. And your heart they have stolen away."

But look again. Yours is a public school. You have the low man on the totem pole, too. The clumsy

beginner fumbling on the bottom rung. Some children always lead, yes, but you also have the little
lost sheep. You have Jack-be-nimble, Jack-be-quick,
but don't forget Clara-the-frump and Peter-who-
clumps. Your children all differ, but each and every
one of them needs to like you. Or, to put first things
first: They need you to like them.

Parents face the same task. A child is born . . .
blind. The new baby is crippled. The new baby has
a cleft palate. The new baby is the eighth girl! But
good parents know: A baby is a baby. A baby must
find good people around him no matter what. The
child is here and that is enough.

Families cannot say: We like only boys . . . or
well children . . . or the smartest one of the pack.
Not without hurting youngsters, not without robbing
them of the basic support every child needs.

Of course families have only one new child every
once in a while. Teachers have a whole litter each
September. The family can concentrate on its one
new product. It can search out the special strength,
the special talent each new offspring bears.

Yours is mass production, but your children must
all share your warmth. Your feeling for them must
let them all say: "She's swell . . . I like her . . .
That's *my* teacher . . . She's good."

Don't take this to mean that you treat all children alike. It is true: *All* your children must like you, not only the successful, fair-haired ones. But some of your class need to like you more than others! Some need more of your time, your friendliness, your good-will. Treat them all the same, and your servings of yourself will be too tiny for some and a tremendous mouthful for others.

Your group includes boys and girls who, by their inherited nature, are more affectionate. They are more in need of warm people, more eager to find good adults to pattern after. This is their way of being. Their greater need is as much a part of them as the color of their eyes or the hair on their heads. Nature builds into every child the necessity to like adults, but she does not use a measuring spoon, giving each an identical dose.

Other boys and girls need you more because of the private lives they have lived: father is dead . . . mother works . . . family is busy . . . parents are stern . . . home is full of older and younger brothers and sisters . . . The reasons can be almost as varied as the genes that go into each human's original self. Like nature, life also does not follow a recipe book—an.exact even teaspoon for every child.

Recognizing differences does not only mean that

you pay attention to each individual. It means that
you pay each individual the attention he needs.

Some Special Social
Conditions

The need for love is ever present. As far as we
know all people seek it, all ages. Certain special
social conditions operate, however, which intensify
this need in many American children. You have to
be aware of these conditions; they bear on the
youngsters who come into your class. Some of your
children may be hit especially hard by them; a few
may be passed over more lightly. You have to know
how this normal need for your friendliness is jacked
up for some individuals because they have been born
in America and in these particular times.

Americans generally have a reputation for being
good to children. The GI abroad is a soft touch; he
cannot look at a hungry youngster without sharing
his candy or his gum. Our soldiers are typical of the
rest of us—they go out to children.

You get an indication of the same kindliness when
you see American mothers and fathers shopping for
a child's birthday—the sky is the limit. At Christmas

nothing is too good. One of the most decent expressions of our Christianity and of our democracy is our relationship with children: We want them to have the best.

Our one trouble is: We are better at giving *things* than giving ourselves! Gifts are fine; we even go overboard on them. But we tend to be niggardly with our time, with our companionship, with personal relationships.

On a scorecard which rates societies on their basic friendliness to young children, you would be surprised to see how far down in the league America stands. We have the outward signs of kindliness. But when you come down to some of the fundamentals we turn out to be almost cruel.

An infant gets his first proof of love through feeding. In America our babies are nursed a shorter period than almost any other place in the world! We bottle-feed more babies. We wean them sooner. We say we love children but we don't go in for the cuddling, holding, mothering that infants understand. We want to get a knife, fork, and spoon in their hands just as soon as we can.

The baby gets real proof of love when adults let him be a baby as long as he wants to be. But we Americans tend to be speed demons. We rush youngsters along the path of growth. We toilet-train our children—or try to—earlier than almost any other people in the world. We fuss at babies (much more than most other societies): Be clean . . . Eat the right way . . . Sleep the right amount, at the right time, in the right place.

All young children get proof of love just from being with other humans, close to them. In some parts of the world the baby is carried on the mother's back. In other parts, on the mother's arm. In still other places the mother or an older sister carries the baby on her hip. Baby and mother, baby and protector, baby and safety go everywhere together, and for months stretching into years.

America is the land of the play pen. Ours is the land of the baby carriage (and you must not rock it). We put baby out in the sun or in his room or in his pen. His crying does not matter; he will stop and get over it . . . so many people think.

Many American mothers and fathers have one supreme worry when their children are young: Don't spoil the baby! People hold themselves back. They pick up their children less than they want to; they play with them less; they comfort them less. A great many parents let their babies cry bitter tears; the child may be hungry or wet or uncomfortable or lonesome. Too many adults believe: "He has to learn sooner or later that we won't dance a jig just because he whines."

One factor in our life is that American women are well educated. They have high standards. Ambitions. Drives. Many mothers have real trouble feeling right about simply relaxing with their babies: nursing them, bathing them, singing to them, playing. In our great productive country even women feel: "I ought to be *doing* something. Just loving a baby is not doing enough." Mothers in many other parts of the world have nothing more important open to them. To be with a child, to hold the youngster, to care for him, is their life.

An additional problem is arising in an increasing number of families: There simply is no time. Mother works. She is out of the house on a job. She has outside interests. Friends. The baby has a substitute—a nurse, a maid, or just some elderly woman who "keeps babies"—but rarely does the substitute do "mothering" with any real enthusiasm. Yet mothering is what very young children need.

Other complex factors are a part of our picture: the large number of homes touched by divorce or separation; the many homes where death, a war death or other calamity, has made the mother the sole support; the many homes forced by the high cost of living, or by high standards and ambition, to have both parents work. You cannot simply pass a law: Mothers! Stay home and love your children.

Comparatively, fathers may be doing a better job than mothers today. Once it was beneath the dignity of a man to have anything to do with his baby; that was woman's work. Once the man was henpecked or a sissy if he looked after his young child. This is not the case any longer.

Many men diaper their youngsters. Many bathe them. Many feel proud as peacocks pushing the baby carriage. You can find men all over the floors of America; they are horses riding youngsters on their backs. Or they are carrying youngsters pig-a-back or playing ride-a-cockhorse. This change is a very promising one and all to the good. The more helping hands in the home, the more running feet, the more people paying attention to baby, the better off the youngster is.

But on the masculine side, too, there have been losses. Men may be more willing to act like fathers, but many of them are running to catch the 7:13. They are commuters, by train or bus or in their own cars. Their work is farther from their homes. Father is brimming with good spirits but the children are asleep when he overflows.

Add to this picture all the disruptions caused by our wars. Many men were in Germany, in Japan, in Korea while their babies were little. And when they came back (or even if they had never been away) earning a living came first. Having fun with baby still plays a poor second in America.

How Do Your Youngsters
Stack Up?

All children start with a deep yearning to know that people are good, that the humans around them will back them up. If this lesson is learned fully at the start of life a youngster need not put quite so much of his emotional energy into worry about people as the days go along.

But never is this lesson learned once and for all. It boomerangs. It comes back afresh at each new age, in each new situation, with each new person. The child with a good start faces his search each time with less panic. The child with a less good start feels it very sharply on each turn around.

You will do well to size up the social conditions

which have been bearing on your children. You can know without fail: Every single one of them will want to find you friendly. For some children, however, your friendliness can be especially important.

You, in Your Classroom

Your youngsters must like you, no matter what age you teach. Only one thing does change: The baby gets his Sense of Trust one way; school-age children are looking for different evidence; older youngsters seek still other signs as the proof of the pudding. All ages search for the same thing, but each age finds what it wants in a different way.

Your Feeling Tone

You have to be smart enough to know how your age conducts its search. You can be sure that the closer children are to infancy the more they will accept the signs the infant does. Nursery school, kindergarten, primary children will click best with someone who is motherly. Not that being motherly means having white hair. Even a man can be "motherly" (and there are some good men teachers of very young children) ! These youngsters want an easy-going way; a patient way that gives them lots of time; a gentle way, relaxed and comfortable. And, although obviously you as a teacher have to act in the way that is right for you, young children almost surely are looking for physical signs that you care: your arm around a child's shoulder, sometimes holding a youngster on your lap, holding a hand, and lots of sympathy when children are hurt . . . or when they think they are hurt.

You know the old song, "I Want a Girl—Just Like the Girl That Married Dear Old Dad." That sums up the way these youngest children will come to think you are the best in the world. You may be only twenty-two, out on your first teaching job, but you have to be a great big mother: warm, tender, knowing each child as if he were your only one.

As children get older they are not looking for a wonderful mother hen. They want you to be a good egg!

They want you to do things with them. The middle elementary school age has a rough-and-tumble quality. They look for some of this in you; you are good if you can take it. These boys and girls are bound and determined to be skilled at something. They size you up through their eyes; you are good if *you* can do things—things that have top billing in children's minds: Can you run? Can you throw a ball? Can you yo-yo? Can you ride a bike or roller skate?

Even these big hulks in fourth and fifth and sixth grade will want some sympathy when they are hurt; you have to be a friendly port if a storm comes along. But, apart from emergencies, companionship best sums up what this age is seeking.

The GI's in Korea voted on a Hollywood starlet who best fitted the description: "The girl I would most want to be shipwrecked with." So, too, these middle elementary children are voting on you. The GI would probably say: "How about a kiss?" These youngsters, boys and girls, are more likely to ask: "How about a catch?"

Still further up on the age scale most young people will be looking for a different sign. They wouldn't want you to hold their hands for all the money in the world, and they don't care too much whether you can do things with them. (Thank heavens they don't. Most of us would look like duffers competing with their skills!) These young people want respect. The one thing they know is that they are not babies any more, they are not children. Their hearts will go out to you if you know this, too.

When you don't hold adolescents off at arm's length then they know that you know they are big. They want you to take them seriously. To talk with them. To look them straight in the eye. To listen to what they have to say. Act this way, then you are O.K. . . . and they feel good, too.

In a sense you are the Membership Committee of a club. The club is "For Adults Only." If you won't let these older boys and girls in, they have only one alternative: They are not going to like you, your club, or anything about you. They want to belong so badly that, when you shut the door, they cover up their hurts by saying nasty things and acting in difficult ways. But the minute you let them join, they will be your most enthusiastic members.

All this may sound like a prescription, but it is not. You cannot go to a charm school to have the prescription filled: six doses and then your children fall in love with you. You exert your greatest charm when you are yourself. We each have our own ways of being friendly, doing what comes naturally to us. When we try to be a "good fellow" but feel like a fish out of water, youngsters usually see through us.

They don't get the true sense they are after, of being with a person who honestly likes them.

Even babies are smart enough to see through people. Mamma can gurgle and coo and go through all the motions, but unless she feels right the baby is worried. But most teachers do feel right. We like children. We get fun out of them. We would not have gone into teaching if we didn't. Our big job is to let our good feelings show through.

The Personal Touch

Once you realize that love is the very basis of learning you will find things to do. Your good feelings will not stay wrapped up inside of you—"Don't open until graduation"—where they cannot do children much good.

For children do not get what they need from strong, silent courtships. Every now and again you read of a couple, seventy years old, who marry after having lived in the same community and gone to the same church for half a century. The groom shyly confesses: "I've loved her ever since third grade but I couldn't find the courage to tell her so." Don't hide your goodwill this way.

You can show it through the personal things you do for youngsters. Then they know you care. One obvious suggestion is to do something for the child who is sick. A youngster in your class fractures his skull or stubs his toe. If you let him know that you feel some of the pain, he will respond. If he is out of your class for a week or a month, and you never ask why or where or how, the youngster understands: He is just a name on your roll, something you put a check mark or a cross after. No boy or girl can fall in love with a pencil.

If you write, if you phone or visit, if you send something to make the illness more bearable, the child knows that in your eyes he is a human. In his eyes you become a more desirable human.

Humans hurt at times. Even young children have sorrows and grief. Humans exult. Even young children have peaks of pride and exhilaration. If you want your youngsters to like you, you have to share some of these high points and depressions with them.

Their pets die. A new baseball glove thrills them. They miss out on a part in a play. Their name gets in the newspaper. You must develop a seismograph of your own, some means of keeping your ear to the ground. You have to know these ups and downs of youngsters. Then you can find your way of saying, "I'm so glad" or "I'm so sorry."

Your conversations with children cannot be confined to "How much is six times nine? How do you spell 'colonial'? What is the biggest river in Latin America?" This is icecube talk. Casual acquaintances fill their conversation with such impersonalities, but a child does not want you to be a passing blob. Some of your relationships must go down to where children's feeling lives are.

You have the personal touch, too, when you work with a child who needs a helping hand. You are Johnny-on-the-spot. You are useful to the youngster.

This is what we do in our adult lives. A family moves in next door; we bring supper over to save them the trouble of cooking. They know we are their friends. A neighbor's car is stuck; we get out and push, we don't stand in the window cheering him on. A friend has a flat tire; we offer a jack, a spare, a patch. We don't stand by full of good advice.

Youngsters have flat tires, too. They get stalled. Pitch in at times like these and you are a friend, you make a friend. Sally would give anything to know how to dance. Bob is all muddled about "borrowing" in subtraction. Beth cannot for the life of her tell an adverb from an adjective. Joe hits nothing but pop flies because he swings his bat so hard. A few minutes of your time, a little personal advice, your focus on the specific thing wearing down this particular child mean you have value in a child's life. Maybe you work with him alone during school hours. Maybe the two of you stay a short time after school. Maybe you make a special date for Saturday. The youngster knows you care.

This is not the same as drill. This is not the same as homework or practice. This is not because you see something the child is doing wrong. This is not your bright idea for making a child do something better. The youngster is in a jam; he knows he is in a jam; he wants to get out of the mess. And you offer to help him. You are not a boss, nagging. You are a friend, helping.

Eagle Eyes Are No Good

Your active courtship makes you find things to do. It also makes you find things *not* to do. Your children will like you if you don't peck at them for every little thing that goes wrong.

Every age of childhood has some rumbles. They are normal and natural, the kinds of noises children

have to make. You become a more likeable person
if you stuff some cotton in your ears. Sharp-pointed
ears don't add to your attractiveness.

Every age of childhood has some smudges and
rumpled spots. They are normal and natural, the
kinds of stains children have to have. You become a
more likeable person if you wear dark glasses. Eagle
eyes, two in front and two in back of your head,
don't add to your attractiveness.

Think about little babies for a moment. Babies
wake up in the middle of the night, and they scream
and howl. Babies wet, and babies even smell at
times. Babies spit up on mothers' new dresses and
fathers' new suits. Babies have to be burped, a most
undignified procedure. Babies are very unsatisfactory
creatures . . . unless you like babies. Then you are
glad to take them the way they come.

You have to like whatever age you teach. You
have to be willing to take them as you find them.
You cannot be satisfied only with white ties and tails.

Youngsters are very sensitive to this. You see it in
every neighborhood. The whole gang is over in the
Browns' TV room; everyone is down in the Browns'
recreation room. The children will tell you: "The
Browns are swell. They understand kids." Your chil-

dren have to want to congregate around you, because you understand.

You can take children: *young children* who
wiggle and interrupt, who get up and wander, who
are noisy and active, who sometimes even seem to
steal because toys and chalk and crayons find their
way into their pockets; *older boys and girls* so boast-
ful and brassy, who complain and gripe, who whisper
and who have maddening giggles, who specialize in
jokes that even Miller's *Joke Book* would scorn;
adolescents who are so overly sensitive, who speak
with such positiveness, who act at times as if the
whole world spun on its little stem around them and
their important wishes.

If youngsters don't get under your skin they will
like you. Your tolerance, your enjoyment of the
things each age does, your appreciation that a youngster is only nine once (and all too soon he is ninety-
nine) make you someone they can turn to.

Some More Specific Suggestions

As teachers most of us don't have to study tech-
niques for letting youngsters know our friendliness.

All we have to do is to persuade ourselves that this is a good way to be. Then our own ideas flow. But a few even more specific ideas may start your thinking going:

1. Keep your eye on youngsters who have the poorest academic record.

2. Watch particularly those boys and girls in your group who get picked on—the ones the other children tease or call names or make fun of.

3. Spot any children who differ: the fat boy and girl, the skinny one, the "brain," the fellow whose interest is stars (heavenly kind), when other youngsters are following the Hollywood variety. These children may especially need a close relationship with you. You cannot pass a law to make the other children like them, but you can like them and they can like you.

4. Ask yourself honestly: What child don't you warm up to? Someone is bound to leave you cold. Unless you do something to change the situation, you will leave the child cold, too. Visit this youngster's home. Take him on a trip. Do something special with him so you get to know him better. An old adage always works: You can't know someone well without coming to like him. Try it out on the youngster you usually avoid.

Discussion Time

Words on paper about human relations tend to
have a flat, final sound. They seem so authoritative.
As you read them you can easily get the impression:
Here is the final answer, the gospel truth. At the
same time the ideas sound deceptively simple. *Your
youngsters must like you:* nothing very technical or
complex about that! Yet, when you move into action
the words begin to wobble. Doubts arise. Questions
pop up.

"Get 'Em Young and Treat 'Em Rough"

Many people wonder, for example, if it is wise to
be too friendly with youngsters from the very beginning of a class. It makes better sense to them to be
strict at the beginning. Let the children know who is
boss, and then loosen up.

Classrooms which operate this way—many do—
seem to come out all right. But from the standpoint
of Child Development this much is clear: Life does
not get off to a good start this way. The mother and
father who set out to be strict with their baby at the

beginning are headed for trouble. The baby gets weaned all right. He finally gets toilet trained. He stops crying. He doesn't fuss when he is left alone. You can look at the child and say: "See. It works." But you don't see the inside of a child. Outside, on the surface, there are no scratches. If you could get inside you might find some hurts.

You cannot always tell what works and what doesn't just by looking at a child.

This is true of adults too. Think about the communist-dominated countries. The people hold jobs. They go home at the end of a day. They raise families. They vote "Yes" in elections. Take a quick look and you may say: "See. It works. The people seem all right." But you know that inside they must be tight, tense, troubled.

Communist countries settle down into order right away. As soon as the party takes over everything looks smooth and in control. Democratic lands have upheavals, conflicts, disagreements. Yet, we think that the former are weak inside, and that the latter have a basic strength and spontaneity and power.

You can get compliance from children. They are so dependent on getting along with adults that you have to push them very hard to produce open rebellion. But there is real reason to think that strictness, sternness, coldness, aloofness never get the best out of a child.

The way people are made, our very nature, means that first in any steady relationship we have to get the feeling: "They are O.K. . . . I am O.K." People don't operate on all their cylinders until that is straightened out. They may do what they are supposed to do, but something else is on their minds. Some of their energies are siphoned off by worry over this basic essential.

There is one other point too: At every age children must make an effort to do what adults want. They have to give up some of their childish ways. To please adults, children must hit less or grab less or talk less or run less or interrupt less or play less than comes easily. A child has to exercise some self-control. No matter what you are like, or how much he likes you, no child can turn into an angel overnight. He is still a child, but he is willing to struggle to come through with the best behavior he is capable of.

From the child's standpoint, the effort is worthwhile when he gets your friendship in return. He feels good about what he is doing. He feels more like trying. He gives up something but he gets a replacement: He likes you, and he is becoming more like you. *But,* unless you have rung a bell with him, un-less he wants to be like you, the child sees little point in making the effort.

He can be good because you make him. But then you do all the work. The other way—*he likes you, he wants to be like you*—is slower. In the long run it is safer, and it lasts.

"They Will Take Advantage of You"

Some people still hesitate. They fear that if they are friendly and easy-going youngsters will take ad-vantage of them. This fear is not entirely ground-less. The children might seem to do just that at first. You have to be prepared for it. Don't be too sur-prised if the first days, weeks, a month, or so—it is hard to tell how long—are a little on the hectic side. This can be particularly true if parents and past teachers have been bossy. When you come along as a friend your children may go overboard for a while.

But not forever.

Children are not against adults. They need adults' goodwill and approval more than anything in the world.

Children are not geared to fighting adults. They have to be on your side. This is what they hunger for.

If their past has taught them that adults are cold, unfriendly, disinterested, they will expect you to be the same. But you smile. Children may take a quick look and think they see an adult with whom they can fight and win. They have fought with other adults and lost. But basically they are not happy either way. They want to work *with* adults. Life is too big and frightening if the adults are on the opposing side, either as winners or losers.

If you are patient . . . if you keep talking things through with children . . . if you are fair . . . if you keep trying to see their side . . . if you keep *saying* your side (not pounding it into them) . . . if you are friendly . . . children will come around. Children have to. They need to feel that adults like them. They need to like adults. The world is not safe for a child unless this is true.

The process takes time. But you get your reward in many ways. When youngsters work because they want to you get more work out of them. When they are good because they want to be you get much better behavior. When the fighting stops—either the open warfare that you may see at first or the guerrilla warfare that past teachers probably haven't seen—

well, peace is wonderful. Your youngsters relax, and you can, too.

"What! Let Them Get Away with Murder?"

This kind of talk sometimes raises a very ugly question. People misunderstand. They seem to believe that being a good scout means letting children get away with murder. If you want your children to like you, they think, you must let them do anything they want to do.

It is hard for some to imagine a middle road in which adults are friendly but still adults. A very flat statement can be one guide: *Youngsters need rules.* They need regulations. They need some standards and expectations. You are no friend to children if you sit back and let the sky be the limit. Don't be confused or hesitant even for a second. In order to have your youngsters feel that you are tops, you do not have to let them run wild.

Child Development can put this kind of statement right out on the table: You do children a favor when you have standards. You hurt them if you don't. Youngsters get the safety they want from you if you stand for an ordered world. You cheat them out of an essential if you mix up friendliness with flabbiness, warmth with wooziness, being a good fellow with being on the same plane as one of the boys.

This should not surprise you because it is part and parcel of what has already been said about infancy. The infant cannot live alone. Babies simply are not sufficient unto themselves. The infant's very survival depends on big, strong mother-father hands that pat him to burp him, that hold his head up straight when the neck muscles are still too weak, that gently turn his head to the side so that he can breathe.

Baby likes it when strong arms pick him up. He likes it when big gentle hands bathe him. He likes it when he can nuzzle close to a big body . . . to nurse, to rest, to sleep. Then he knows he is safe. The world would be overwhelming and frightening to a little child—no Sense of Trust anywhere in it—without good, big people to turn to.

From the very start of life friendliness equals just being there, being on hand, a supporter. Babies don't get love through long-distance telephone calls or by having the word spelled out in a telegram. The sure adult, the pillar, is Love. The child can feel it, turn to it, press it close, bury himself in it when thunder is loud or when the ear hurts or when the television show is too frightening.

The meaning is clear for every age. Be friendly, sure. Be warm and approachable. Be decent, *but* be an adult. Children want you to be. They need someone stronger than they are—more aware, more alert —as a prop to their own efforts to do the right thing.

Youngsters don't want rules staring them in the face wherever they turn. They don't want to be picked up on every little thing they do every second of the day. They appreciate a little flexibility. If the same law is broken time and time again they hope you will take a second look at the rule to see if it really is a good one.

They want some patience on your part. You cannot pass a law and expect children to be letter-perfect on it the very next second. Children need time to learn how to do the right thing, the way it takes them time to learn to read or to do arithmetic or to learn a declension in Latin. You have to allow some leeway for mistakes in behavior, just as you allow time for mistakes in grammar to straighten out. The heavens must not fall every time there is a slip.

Youngsters like it best, too, when you talk things over and keep talking them over, day after day. If you are harsh, you push children away from you. If you are severe, you push them back. If you are tough, you push them off. When you explain, interpret, discuss, then you draw the youngsters in.

If you have a rule, if it is a good rule, stick by it. Your sensible, reasonable rule joins hands with the friendly talking way you uphold the rule. The two together—your rule and your friendliness—develop strength and security in youngsters.

"But Some Ages Are Anti-Adult"

Some people reading this are sure to think of ages they know when children seem to fight rules and regulations. It is one thing to say that youngsters want to be on the adults' side. Yet, when you see the children, particularly in some grades, they act as if they were *anti*-adult.

At certain ages youngsters do sound as if they were off adults for life. Most typically you hear this noise as youngsters move into preadolescence. If you teach in the upper elementary school or in junior high, don't take it too hard if youngsters are slower to warm up to you. And don't be hard on yourself if the youngsters are a little hard on you.

This age is walking away from childhood. They are striking out on their own. Just a short time ago these boys and girls were dependent, and they wanted to be. Now they are feeling big, and they put on quite a show of it.

A lot of the noise you hear at this time is static, however. These youngsters put on a pose of objecting, even when they don't feel too unhappy. Keep in mind that their bark is worse than their bite.

Down underneath preadolescents are like any other age. They want to like you, they want you to like them, and they want some rules to keep them on the straight and narrow. They talk big. They gripe. They may hold you off at arm's length for a while. They live in their own little world and seem to shut you out. When you first see the age you can believe that a real battle is going on between children and teachers. Actually it is just a friendly tug-of-war!

This age *talks* big and tough and "anti" but it *acts* reasonably well. Once these youngsters find that you can laugh, that you can take a joke, that you are not falling apart at the seams, they are very prepared to like you—more so than many another age.

These boys and girls are in the same conflict with

their parents as they are with you. They are trying
to break away a bit and to be more on their own. If
you can keep cheerful you will do them a big favor.
Basically they are eager to find a real friend outside
the home. Once they find that friend—it can be you
—they have taken a tremendous step forward in
their development.

3

Your Youngsters Must Like Their Work

When you are friendly you turn the air-conditioners on. The climate is right. You tone down the distractions. Your children like you so the working conditions are good. Now you are ready to teach.

Child Development says: Teach right down your children's alley.

Hit them where they live.

Put the ball over home plate.

Hit the mark and ring the bell.

Your youngsters—each and every one of them—must feel successful.

The Child Development
Background

The need for warm, satisfying relationships with good adults keeps a high priority with all of us through all our days. But people grow, and people change. By the time a child starts to school a new kind of satisfaction has an equally high rating.

The school-going youngster wants to feel that he *can do.* He wants to learn. He wants to know more. He wants to become skilled. School must be the place where he learns to look upon himself as able, as competent, as an adequate person who has something to give.

With this sense of achievement inside of them children go on to learn more and more. Success gives learning a peanuts-and-popcorn flavor: The more you eat, the more you want. But the growing person —five, six; fifteen, sixteen—who does not like his work has a flat and bitter taste in his mouth. His appetite is gone.

Toward the "Real McCoy"

A change takes place about school-starting time. Look back for a moment at the preschool child. He plays with a box on his playground. The box is a plane or a boat, a firehouse or an apartment house, a hill, a railroad train, a garage . . . yet the box is a box is a box. The Three, the Four, the Five lives his fullest life inside of himself. The outside world is there but only for him to use, to change, to shape to suit his private purposes.

The young child makes up his own game. You hear him say: "I must be the doctor and you must be sick." "I must be the grocery man and you must want to buy something." Someone else's rigid rules have no place in his play life: Three strikes and you are out. . . . Nine innings make a game . . . No running on a foul. The young child's rules are all within his own mind, and they change from minute to minute.

Under six, the child paints a picture. It need not look like anything. At the drop of a hat he will tell you a long involved story about it. A few minutes later he can tell you another story, just as good as the first one. But the time comes when he is bothered if the paint runs. As the years go on the picture has to look like the real thing. The child becomes sternly critical of himself, so severe and so demanding that for a while he may not paint at all. His work—even when now he labors over it—cannot come up to his new standards.

The movement of development is all toward reality. The little two-year-old boy thinks nothing of putting on girl's clothing; a hat, skirt and heels are wonderful for dress up. The ten-year-old boy would not be found dead looking like a girl.

The five-year-old holds the ball and fondles it. He laughs when he throws backwards over his shoulder —chasing the ball makes the game even more fun. The ten-year-old is irritated: "Don't make love to the ball. Throw it!"

The four-year-old dances to the music, all "airy-fairy." Every step is a new one, never danced before. The fourteen-year-old makes jitter-bugging a ritual. Each step must be exactly right, the way everyone else does it.

The three-year-old hammers a nail into wood; he has a delightful boat. The thirteen-year-old struggles with his model—it must be an exact replica. The two-year-old pushes a block along the floor; he has a perfect train. The twelve-year-old dreams of an electric motor for his coal-loader, automatic signals at the crossings, and a railroad station complete with a baggage room and a drinking fountain!

No curtain drops at year Six. No one single dramatic change takes place. But gradually, as children move into our public schools, the real world becomes more important to them. Building blocks satisfy less. The child is headed for an Erector set; then what he makes can work and look real. Tossing a football back and forth, kicking it to see how high it will go, merges into touch football. Slowly even that fades. "Let's play tackle"—that's the real McCoy.

A successful life—a job really done, a skill really learned, an objective accomplished—is the life the school-age child wants. There are not too many dreams in this life. Not much slap-dash. This age goes for the hard, critical measuring of the self against the demands of reality.

Not Anything Goes

Knowledge, facts, skills, answers are the school child's meat. Developmentally, youngsters come to you looking for all these to chew on. But you must keep one rigid, stark, stubborn fact in mind: At every age—no matter how young or old—youngsters can learn to do some things, but they cannot master others. Not because they won't try. Not because they are lazy. Not because they want the easy way out. Not because teachers today are soft and you do not force your students enough.

Youngsters can succeed if they have grown sufficiently to master the job: Their minds must grow, their nervous systems, their bones and muscles and organs, their bodies as a whole. Youngsters are doomed to fail if their organisms need still more time to mature.

There you have another flat statement. Think of it as a law if you want to. But you cannot repeal this law. And you cannot get around it or overlook it or cheat on it. This is not a man-made law or some recent hurried legislation. This rule is written for keeps, deep down in the very bodies of your youngsters.

Most of us know this law. We obey it, particularly when some physical act is involved. Then we are patient. We are willing to grant, "He isn't old enough yet" . . . to learn how to catch a ball, to go down steps one foot at a time, to use a knife to cut his meat, to button his own buttons. No one has to tell us that about six years of growing must pass before a youngster loses his front baby teeth. Girls and boys need time to grow out of childhood before breasts develop and pubic hair grows. We know this. We are in no rush. The youngsters can have the time. We can't see any wheels turning inside but we have faith: The wheels must be there, and they must be turning . . . in these physical areas.

You have to be just as sure: There are intellectual wheels, too. Social wheels. Emotional wheels. Memory wheels. Reasoning wheels. Attention-span wheels. This law of growth does not apply only to physical changes. It controls and governs almost everything the child can do and can't do. It determines the development of his mind and of his body as a whole, not simply his muscles.

Most people can accept this idea more easily when they apply it to younger children—infants and babies. "Don't wean him yet; he's too young." "Don't try to toilet train him so early; let him grow a little more." "It's too soon to give him solid foods; he can't manage them yet. Wait a little while." "Don't fuss at him for crying; that's all you can expect a little baby to do." "Sure, he's unsteady on his feet; he's only fourteen months old—give him a chance."

But the law is not some special law passed for the benefit of little ones only. It applies to school-age youngsters just as much; to adolescents; to the college age and to adults. This is not like Daylight Saving; the time limit does not expire on a certain day of a certain month. Whether you are teaching algebra or grammar; a unit on farm animals or on the community's health protection; whether you are looking at second-graders pushing at the drinking fountain or at high school boys hanging around the Coke machine, the same basic rule applies.

A Strong Chain

Children inherit their rate of growth. At the moment of their conception the speed at which they will mature is bred into them. As soon as the two cells join, a child's own particular private horsepower is established. The way you treat the youngster can lower his capacities. You can make him function on only three of his four cylinders or on seven of his eight. But you cannot build an extra cylinder into him. A youngster has to be himself.

Get the force of this. A child is the product of his

mother and father. He inherits from them the genes which set the pace for his rate of development. But he inherits, too, from grandmothers and grand-fathers: two on each side of the family. What each of them was like has a bearing on how fast this child will grow. Now put into this picture the contributions of great-grands—four this time on each side—and great-great-grands before that. You see an endless chain stretching forever back. This chain of inher-itance sets each child's speed. This chain has the power, not the child. A youngster simply must be himself.

Think how you would feel—women reading this —if you were constantly urged to be men. "Change!" But you can't. "Be different!" But you can't. "Be something other than yourself!" It is impossible.

Think how you would feel—men reading this—if you were constantly urged to have gills. "Grow them!" But that is out of the question. "Will them!" But you have no power to.

The child cannot be speeded up, no more than you can change your sex or your kind. When you high-pressure a child you make him feel like a worm, low-down and no good. You hurt the child. That simply is not decent.

The Time Will Come

Wait and you will have permission soon, permission from this chain that controls the child's growing. The time will come when the child is ready.

Look at a two-year-old. Reading does not mean a thing to him. He passes billboards, and he does not see them. He passes street signs, and they have no meaning. Road markers? Danger signs? Labels on boxes? They might just as well not be there as far as the two-year-old is concerned.

Read the three-year-old a story. He likes to listen, but the process of reading does not concern him in the slightest. Do you have a technique? Do you use magic? The problem simply does not exist for him. Any more than you puzzle over whether it hurts when one speck of sand tumbles on another in the middle of the Gobi desert. Just as long as you read— that is enough for the three-year-old.

The same is true of most four-year-olds, of most Fives. They cannot yet see well enough. They cannot yet think well enough. They feel no problem, no interest, no concern. Reading is the other fellow's job. Just the way, if you live in New York, you don't think about that lawnmower that needs fixing in the backyard of a frame house in Lida in Esmeralda County in southwest Nevada.

No matter how much *you* love reading and think it is important—your best bet is to let these children grow some more. Time passes and their minds mature. Their bodies develop. Their brain cells, their thinking powers, their ability to remember, their capacity to see. The child does not do anything to bring this about. He isn't trying or not trying. He is not making any effort. Nor must you make an effort. The youngster is growing.

The same silent process goes on that earlier made a tooth break through; that changed the color of the eyes from newborn baby blue to their present brown; that put a shock of black hair on the youngster's head where once there was only blond baby fuzz.

You cannot see the wheels turn inside but they are turning all the time. With babies: Yesterday he only gurgled but today he says a real word. With thirteen-month-olds: Yesterday he simply stood and rocked back and forth; today he took an honest-to-goodness step . . . and then fell down! With thirteen-year-olds: Yesterday all she would wear were jeans; today she complains because you never buy her any dresses.

The time will come with reading. Some day the youngster will want to know: "Where does it say 'cowboy'?" Some day he will say: "Show me where it says my name." Some day he will pester his mother or his teacher: "In 41, does the 4 come first or the 1?"

Slowly, Gradually

The child is growing and the problem is *beginning* to be real to him. Some sand from the Gobi desert has blown in his eye; he is starting to notice that lawnmower out in Esmeralda County. But the start is a slow start. Don't forget: That first tooth took weeks to come through, and it was months before the baby had a full crop of hair. The baby is not ready yet for a toothbrush, and he does not yet need a home permanent wave. Nor is this fellow, taking his first little steps toward reading, craving an encyclopedia.

Development is a slow process. You have to be patient. You cannot make more teeth come by rubbing the gums, and the hair won't grow faster if the child stares at Daddy's bushy mop. The youngster is not the boss here, or even the worker. He cannot decide to speed up and he cannot decide to work

overtime. Growth is the boss. Time is the worker—
time the cells need to mature.

You cannot spurt ahead just because you see the
merest flicker of a green light. The child did say
"Mama" once in the morning; that does not mean
that now you can teach him Lincoln's Gettysburg
Address. By six o'clock the child will be back to his
gurgling, not saying anything that sounds like a
word. Ask fathers, they know!

The youngster at the very start of reading may
devil you to show him words; then for days he will
want you simply to read and not stop. He may write
his name perfectly for a while; then he spells the
whole word backwards with every letter going the
wrong way. He may forget words—just draw a
blank—when you thought he knew for sure. The
more important the goal is to you the more you have
to hold your horses. You cannot wait a decent inter-
val and then say: "Here we go, ready or not."

We are apt to get all excited about the one new,
tender, little shoot popping its head through the
ground—particularly if it is the flower we love. But
think about a child who has just taken his first step.
For months someone will still have to carry him. For
months he is still going to crawl. For months someone will still have to lift him and haul him and hold

him by the hand. He can walk, but he is not a walking child.

Suppose you said to a baby: "Now you have your first tooth. From here on we are going to feed you only steaks." Your poor baby would shrivel up and die.

Imagine saying this to the thirteen-year-old who wanted a dress: "You are getting interested in boys, are you? All right. From now on you can only go with boys. No girl friends. You have to grow up." The poor girl would shrivel up and die, too. At eighteen she might kiss you on both cheeks for dreaming up such a wonderful idea, but at thirteen you would frighten her to death.

And you do frighten children or bore them or worry them or hurt them if you see only the tender new shoot. The youngster has some interest in reading, but he is not yet a reading child. The fourth-grader has some interest in the past, but he is not yet an antiquarian. The high-schooler has some ability to cope with generalizations, abstractions, and symbols—but he is far from being a philosopher.

Children are like turtles. If you concentrate on skills they are just beginning to master, or cannot do at all, they yank their heads back into their shells. But the time will come. Some day parents will have to pull the child's nose out of a book. They will have to yell: "Stop reading, turn out the light, and go to bed" or "Finish your reading later. Now you have to set the table."

Some day the steak will taste good. The child will walk, too; in fact he will skip and run and jump and gallop. After a while boys will seem like quite nice creatures—too bad the school does not have more of them.

The Time Is Always Now

But don't think of the law of growth as a negative law. If your heart is set on teaching some very favorite learning, you may well have to wait. But this law is not basically a prohibition. It is permission.

The most important clause—the key to good living with youngsters—is the first clause: Children *could do* some things because they *have* grown sufficiently to do them. Growth has no blank spots. Never a void. Children *always* are ready to learn. Always some achievements—good and worthwhile and important—are possible. Trees lie dormant.

Seeds do. Spores do. Bears hibernate. But children, *never*.

Don't sell short even the very beginner just because he cannot yet learn algebra or long division. The babe in the crib is ready to learn . . . to grasp better, to see more, to hold, to lift his head and to bear it more steadily, to reach. A child is never too young to learn.

Granted that five-year-olds have not yet grown enough to be able to read. That is no cause for gloom. Look at all they can do because they have lived as long as Five: They have active tongues. They can ask for information. Nothing is wrong with their eyes. They can go places and see for themselves. Their hands are in good working order. Their feet function all right. Their bodies are in good shape. These children are ready to become magnificent firsthand scholars.

A six-year-old looks at a word on the blackboard and is as unresponsive as a cantaloupe. Let him look at a drop of water through a microscope. That is important learning, too, and now the child is thrilled. A six-year-old struggles, weary and bored, to make a pencil go where it should, between the lines and nice and round. Put a brace and bit in that child's hands. He will come to life and really work.

You never have to feel sad because children are the way they are. The time is always now. *Now* you can teach certain things. Nines can learn *this,* and they will want to. Thirteens can learn *this,* and they will want to. Seven-year-olds can learn *this,* and they will want to. March through all the doors that are open to you, and your children will know success.

Some Special Social Conditions

America's hard-headed practicality gives a great deal of support to this way of living with children. A business-like America finds it easy to say: "Don't waste your time . . . teach what children are ready to learn." A common-sensical America finds it easy to say: "Don't butt your head against a stone wall . . . teach what children are ready to learn."

Homes are doing this perhaps more than schools are. Many parents are doing what, in good USA language, is nothing else but the efficient thing: They are waiting to wean until the baby is ready; they are waiting to toilet-train until the baby is ready; they are holding off on table manners until the child is ready. This kind of efficiency gives children a good break.

In these years before six many children are equally the beneficiaries of the opposite side of the coin: Their parents concentrate on what these children *can do*. More and more youngsters have blocks to play with. More and more at home have clay and finger paints and easel paints. They have toy trucks and trains and boats and planes. Their backyards are filled with boxes and boards, with climbing apparatus and swings. These children are being helped to learn how to play together.

They are having experiences which develop their attention span, their imagination, their resourcefulness, their problem-solving ability. Young children are very ready for these important learnings. They eat up their play, they love it, they learn so effortlessly they do not know they are learning. An America which prides itself on having its feet on the ground tends to look on this approach to childhood as the most logical, obvious, and sensible thing to do. This practical strand in all Americans is a potential support of the schools' efforts to concentrate on what children *can do*.

You can give a fancy name to such efforts. They add up to showing respect for the child's personality. When you think of it that way, you get support from another and perhaps even more basic part of

American life. Both our political beliefs and our common religious attitudes put respect for personality uppermost.

This typically American ethical point of view has helped to change many of our ways of dealing with children. More and more youngsters, at home and in their communities, are busy on activities they enjoy, simply because this way seems the decent way to most adults. Philosophically we have no stake at all in force-feeding our children. Our inclinations are all toward being tolerant rather than pushing people around.

Perhaps the best single illustration comes from the dinner table. More and more parents are not forcing spinach or milk or liver down children's unwilling throats. More and more are not insisting that a child must eat every single speck of food on his plate. More and more are not serving a meal as if they were issuing an ultimatum: "We will fight it out on this line if it takes all summer."

Parents keep looking for what children like to eat. Good parents and wise parents know that this is more than peanuts and popcorn, lollypops and ice cream. Food is good, and children like it. If Billy does not like milk, he likes puddings or creamed soups. If he does not like beets, he likes cabbage. If he does not like liver, he likes egg yolks.

Meals take on a more pleasant tone. In more homes they have become enjoyable, not a three-times-a-day ordeal. And this is symbolic. In many activities parents have no urge to insist and demand in the face of children's resistance, just for the simple sake of winning a battle. As they learn to watch their children they find that if one door is closed another is wide open. And the first door will open later on as the child grows.

At Sixes and Sevens

Two poles—our ethics and our marketplace—support the idea that every child must find success. We like to have a youngster learn early that there is something worth while he can do. But a great many other forces, just as typically American, pull and yank and tug at this idea.

We are highly competitive people, as one example. We have a strong urge to keep up with the Joneses—and maybe even beat them out. This can be very hard on children. Each of us keeps looking out of the corners of his eyes: How are we doing? Are they catching up? Are we holding our own? Are we still ahead?

We are competitive, and we are mobile. Everybody is in the race. Plumbers, ditch diggers, small-store clerks: No one can stand on the sidelines and watch with lukewarm interest. We are all running somewhere. We are trying to get *in*. We may make the country club, or the downtown city club. We may become sales manager or seventeenth vice-president.

The most non-American activity is lack of activity. You have to have ambition. You have to want the best (or the biggest or the newest or the loudest), even if it kills you. Every generation is striving to outdo its forebears: to live in a better part of town, to work in a more white-collar job, to give its children a higher education.

Children are in on the race. They carry our colors. We hold bets on them. We enter them. We train them. And with the best of intentions sometimes we dose them with "shots" to speed them up. In one area of instruction only—the area of sex education—are we content to relax. There we think it is completely right to wait until children ask. Sometimes they have to ask in a very loud voice before we hear them! But in almost every other area the tendency is to rush things.

We like children who are very mannerly . . . early. We like children who read . . . early. We like children who sit quietly . . . early. The pull on all of us—parents as well as teachers—is not to concentrate on what children can do *now* (we focused on that yesterday!) but on what they will be able to do tomorrow. Today gets lost in the shuffle.

Shoving children along the path of growth ties in with our good American interest in speed. We want our cars to have more and more horsepower. We pride ourselves on getting any job done quickly: building a bridge, building a highway, building a hospital, building a bomb. Our difficulty comes because the challenge in development is not to produce an adult in jig-time. The big task is to let a child be a child.

The swift and the fleet always thrive on races, but a great many youngsters you teach come in potato sacks. Races are hard on the hobbled and the slow— the Ferdinands who like to smell the flowers along the way. They are hard on tortoises who will reach the end but in their own sweet time. Races are hard on those who like to stop and stand to see the sun set. Races do not allow time for dabbling your feet in cool mountain water or for skipping pebbles across the pond or watching a leaf spin around in an eddy.

We Americans also tend to be perfectionists. Our products have to come up to some uniform standard or out they go. Mexico turns out its hand-blown glasses, each one a slightly different size. We make our glassware in factories. If we find the slightest imperfection we throw the glass away or sell it cheap as a "second." The American Indians weave ties that are highly prized; each one is different from the other. But tie factories want every tie to be the same. It is one thing to throw away a bowl that is not up to standard. You cannot throw away a child or treat him as a "second."

Many youngsters could do beautifully if only they were entered in the right kind of race. Some could win if the race were for shinnying up a pole. Some could win if it were a swimming race or a hopping race. At home and in schools we are more likely to have just one race: a straight track, hard and fast. You have to run this race to win.

Our problem is to keep these facts and forces in their right places. You want perfectionist standards if you are buying a car. You want speed if someone is building a house for you. Uniformity lets you buy your groceries with confidence; you can go by the brand name and count on it. Competition means you can pick up a bargain when the downtown department stores have a price war. You can be glad you live in America where all these strengths abound.

But a school is a school. A home is a home. The values of the business world do not necessarily hold true when the task is to grow strong humans. You have to sort values out in your mind, and we all have to help parents sort them out, also. Too many children grow up not liking their work, not liking their life, because they are rushed or compared or pressured.

A Saving Grace

As one counteraction to these dangers we have a blessing in disguise today, a boon for children although hard on teachers: Today's youngsters are more like tigers than worms. If you miss the mark with them they are not apt to curl up and shrivel. They will let you know. Youngsters today fight for what is important to them.

This is annoying to adults. But what else could you expect from the children of a free people?

Suppose you lived in Russia. If the state-owned store did not carry the merchandise you wanted would you complain to the manager? Hardly. You would purr like a kitten and keep on coming back to the state-owned store. But not in America, thank you.

In Russia if you thought that your leaders were not serving you would you stand on a caviar box and shout: "Throw the rascals out!"? You would look faithful as a puppy and vote "Yes" at every election. But not in America, thank you.

We have our troubles but we think they are worthwhile. If one store does not sell what we want we go someplace else. If the administration is not doing a good job we say, "Time for a change." If one job does not pay enough we quit and go to work for someone else. Gradually we have been bringing up our children to behave the same way.

There was a time when any adult was the boss. A child was expected to be all respect: quiet, polite, attentive, listening, face glowing and hands on the desk. Women were supposed to know their place, too. And workers were supposed to stay in their place. And poor people. And servants. And everybody.

Everybody had a place, so children were not the only ones. Many examples were set for them. The acquiescent person—whether child or apprentice or clerk or employee or maid—had a lot of support. Many other people were in the same boat. Yet it is hard to believe that children were not rebelling inwardly.

For better or worse this place-knowing is changed, or changing. People are people. They are free. They have a right to come and go, to choose, to decide. To prefer or to abstain. To enthuse or to be indifferent. To leave when they are bored. To buy the other fellow's wares. Even children are people.

Boys and girls come into your classroom wanting to like you. They expect to like you, but you have to be useful to them. They want to work, they expect to work with you, but yours has to be work worth doing in a child's eyes. Youngsters expect to get some satisfaction from it.

Whether good or bad, our children will never again stand in simple awe of an adult. The fact that you are a teacher doesn't make you Henry VIII. Either you have something that children's growth lets them use, or they will go elsewhere.

Don't ever think they can't go away. If they are of school age they will stay in your room, but tune you out; or switch to another channel; or simply go deaf, the way many people do when the commercials start. You already know what happens when youngsters

reach the legal school-leaving age: They go . . .
the way you walk out of a store when the clerk tells
you he does not have a rubber-coated non-dripping
watering can for a purple flower in the size you want.

If you don't like this state of affairs, blame it on
mothers, fathers, policemen, postmen, doctors,
plumbers, grandparents, store clerks, bus drivers. For
years everyone has been talking to little children. We
have been playing with them, laughing with them.
We have all been friendly.

We have let youngsters crawl on the living room
floor. We have displayed them when company came.
We have brought their high chairs up to the table—
we wanted them to eat with us, listen to us, talk to us.

We have let little children pull the papers out of
wastepaper baskets. We picked up their blocks when
they threw them out of the crib, and we handed
them back to be thrown out again. We let them talk
when they thought they had something to say. We
have spanked them less. We have answered their
questions, and we have tried to explain and to tell
them "Why."

You cannot stop something like this. Every little
thing everyone does with a child is a part of the
process. Just saying "Hello" to a youngster, instead
of ignoring him, is it. Letting the child answer a

question, instead of answering for him, is it. Not talking about the child when he is right in front of you is still another way freedom grows. The youngster comes to look upon himself as a person, not a lump or a glob or a thing. Today's free child may seem like a nightmare to some. In reality he is right in line with America's dream.

You may think that today's freer child is harder to teach. Not so! Yesterday's child was quiet but that did not make him read any earlier. He was more passive but that did not make him spell any earlier or add or write or generalize any earlier. It did not make him pay attention any longer or remember any quicker. Fear can change a child's outward behavior but it cannot change the inside of children. It cannot make cells mature or bones grow or a nervous system develop.

Fear does keep children from showing adults how bored they are, how cold, how uninterested. The free child is easier to teach because he lets you know. He sends you signals you can use as a guide. Cowed, quiet children keep you in the dark; you never know what is really going on. The freer child's behavior becomes a gauge. You can tell where you stand.

You, in Your Classroom

Full employment is what you are after in your classroom. Everybody busy, everybody working: the banker, the steamfitter, the poet, and the plumber. No doles. No breadlines. There is no such thing as unemployment compensation for boys and girls—nothing can make up for being idle.

Your people want to work. But they each have their own nine-o'clock whistle. And each whistle has a different sound. You have to keep your ears open so you can hear each one when it blows. Child Development can help you know what to listen for.

Rough Estimates of Growth

When a baby has lived long enough inside of its mother and is ready to be born, the mother can tell. The doctor makes a rough estimate, but only the mother knows for sure. Labor pains begin. Mother knows: Now is the time to be off to the hospital.

When a baby's tooth is ready to come through the gums, the baby can tell (and he wastes no time in letting you know, too). A book gives you a rough idea as to when teeth usually erupt, but the baby knows for sure. He hurts, he howls, and everyone then is certain that now is the time.

When a boy or a girl has grown enough to enter puberty, outward signs inform you. A book gives you the range of years when this growth is apt to take place, but no book tells you about Sam or Suzie in particular. The children's bodies do, however. Pubic hair grows . . . breasts develop . . . menstruation begins . . . voices change.

If only, whenever a child was ready, there could be a pain or a howl or a sore or a bump!

Most of the changes going on inside of children are silent ones, deep ones, down far inside. Even if you could put children under a microscope, or listen with a stethoscope, you still could not spot the changes. It is not simple to tell how mature each child is.

In schools we do what the doctor does: We make a rough estimate. "Children start to learn to read in first grade." "Algebra is a good subject for the first year of high school." "The time to teach cursive writing is about the middle of the third grade."

Then we make believe that the approximation is more exact than it really is. The rough estimate changes from a great big span to a little, fine pinpoint. You can imagine what would happen if a pregnant mother relied too conscientiously on the doctor's rough estimate. The doctor figures that the baby is due about Tuesday. If the mother forgets the "about" and all the other qualifications, bright and early on Tuesday she goes to the hospital but . . . nothing happens! We have to guard against exactly that in schools. Too often nothing happens!

As long as you don't narrow these rough estimates down—trying to pinpoint particular days or weeks or months or even grades—they can serve you well. They keep you in a helpful state of preparedness, like the pregnant mother who has her bags packed, her arrangements made with the taxicab, the doctor, and the hospital.

Once you make the general guides too definite, then preparedness is no longer the word for your state of mind. *Anxiety* is. You become jittery, worried, tense. You put pressure on youngsters for accomplishments they cannot yet do. The children become jittery, worried, tense too.

Keep in mind that the baby knows most about when it is time to be born. He is the only one who can tell whether he has grown enough. In school the child still is the one—he has to tell you whether he has grown enough.

The school youngster does not think out his growth

plans, any more than the unborn infant gets a bright idea: "Today is a good day. Watch me. I will be born." The school youngster does not put his growth into words. He does not ponder about his development and he cannot choose the time, either to push it ahead or to delay it a while. Growth makes the actual decision: a process which neither child nor adult can touch.

But you have to keep your eye on the child to see it. You cannot be looking at a calendar. You cannot be looking at an average. You have to watch each individual.

Listen!

Something like a bell does ring. Something like a pain does begin to hurt. Something like the swelling of gums does begin to show. You do not have to work totally in the dark. There is a sign, an outward sign, that can help you.

What is it? Children's interest. When youngsters are enthusiastic about what is going on, you can be sure that they have grown enough. When they are apathetic, bored, and unresponsive, you have to wonder seriously: Am I ahead of them? Too far ahead? Am I asking for more than they can yet do?

Or am I behind, and they are waiting for me to catch up?

You can see interest. If it is there it shows: *on children's faces*—they are watching and they are eager; *on children's tongues*—they ask questions, they chip in information, they volunteer, you don't have to drag ideas out of them; *on children's ears*—they listen, they even eavesdrop, the ears are pointed and not flapping down. Interest shows, too, *in the time children give*—they have a lot of it, they do not try to break away; and *in children's memories*—you do not battle constantly against forgetting. Youngsters cannot act eager and alive unless their bodies have grown enough.

Interest is not a luxury. It is not a convenience. It is not an incidental. Interest is a fundamental. It is a gauge that shows when your timing is right, when your teaching gears mesh with a child's growth. When interest is in the air, then you know that ideas are about to be born.

Don't confuse interest with agreeability. Interest is strong and forceful. Your youngsters are not dragging their feet. Agreeability is a namby-pamby state; it makes boys and girls say: "O.K., I guess . . . I suppose so . . . If you want to. . . ." But they are not on fire.

Don't confuse interest with acquiescence. Interest equals alive children, giving and putting out. Acquiescence is the same as stiffly polite children; they are present—and that is all you can say.

Watch a one-year-old who has grown enough to walk. You cannot keep him down. He is up on his feet every single chance he gets.

Listen to a one-year-old who has grown enough to talk. He jabbers and jabbers and jabbers. His mouth is open every minute.

Look at a one-year-old who has grown enough to use his hands. He picks up everything he touches. Nothing is safe.

This *doing* and everlastingly wanting-to-do is what you are after, when you cannot hold youngsters back . . . when there is no stopping them . . . when they cannot get enough. You can get this response in reading, in arithmetic, in science, in history, in whatever you teach . . . if your timing is right. When a child's whole body is ready he goes on a jag. If you have to be the one—not the child—to say, "Enough for now," then you can be sure you are in tune with growth.

Everlastingly on the Go

One important reminder to help you stay in tune: Don't forget that, for a long span of years, children must be active. If your way of teaching lets them be on the go—physically and mentally, with their hands and feet and with their tongues and minds—the two of you are sure to harmonize.

This urge for activity is not a minor passing whim, something that kindergarten teachers have to cope with. It is not a little peculiarity you can handle in a recess time. Activity is childhood's brand, its trademark.

You don't have to hunt for this mark. It is out in the open, all over the child at birth. Touch a newborn any place, and he will wiggle all over. Any sensation from outside shoots through him as if he were an empty hall; it meets no resistance anywhere. Touch his hand, and his foot moves; show him a rattle, and his legs move.

The power to hold back—to localize, to keep in— is always in the process of growing. Two-month-olds have it more than one-month-olds; five-year-olds have more than Threes; ten-year-olds much more than Sixes. But long years of growing are needed before the nervous system fully matures so that the human does not have to throw all of himself into everything that comes along every minute of the time.

The whole elementary school age is still close to the beginning of this long journey. Junior high and senior high years may be over the half-way mark but they are not yet at the end. Each day means more time for growth, but you can't expect a youngster to do a lifetime of living in just a few years.

If you teach three-year-olds you know that they have to be on the go. They have to run, jump, touch, feel, talk, move freely, say what comes into their minds. They thrive on a minimum of sitting, a minimum of waiting, a minimum of quiet, a minimum of letting the other fellow do it, a minimum of words . . . a maximum of deeds.

Four-year-olds are the same.

Five-year-olds, ditto.

You often see a kindergarten room as big as a bowling alley. Then first grade rooms, second grade, third grade, and fourth slump to shuffle board size. But gout and arthritis do not set in this early in people.

Six-year-olds are as active as Fives . . . and they are bigger, noisier, they move more quickly. Seven-year-olds, eight-year-olds . . . the activity line is going down but it is not even at midpoint yet.

Look at ten-year-olds. They would rather play a baseball game of their own than watch the World Series on television. They would rather throw a football than see the Army-Navy game. Invite a ten-year-old to go with you for a Sunday drive. "Who wants to just sit?" is his answer.

Who wants to sit? The time will come. The human grows so that he can sit . . . and listen . . . and take notes. The time will come. The human grows so that he can limit his responses to thinking and reflection. But even high-schoolers have not yet reached this sedate anemic and academic stage. Adults can settle down in their seats. Boys and girls go to sleep when they do it. Someone else's tongue wagging is not enough activity to keep them alert.

Every age does not have to run and shout. Nor is activity the equivalent only of hammering and working with clay. Committee work is activity. Discussion is activity. Panels and reports. First-hand research is excellent activity. Experimentation is.

You find the right level of activity for the age you teach, no matter what the age; but keep clearly in mind: Youngsters are *verb* creatures. They are action people. *Doing* souls. Their verbs must have a rugged vital quality to them, or this life is not for them. *Read* is a verb, *recite* is a verb, but pale verbs and too feeble. Children want to do more with their facts than store them. They want to do more with their skills than save them. They want to do more with knowledge than study it.

"Child" Has a Capital "I" in the Middle

Child Development can offer you a second basic guide for keeping in tune with growth. Youngsters of all ages must see themselves in what they are doing. They have to identify the importance to *them,* the significance to *them,* the meaning to *them,* of whatever is going on.

The infant is totally greedy. He is a selfish, grabbing, "what's-in-it-for-me?" kind of person. Long years of growing pass before he is able to care: "What's happening to the other fellow?"

The infant lives for today, this moment now. Long years of growing must pass before he is able to know that there was a yesterday and to conceive of a tomorrow.

The infant has "Home Town Boy" written all over him. This place (his crib, his room) and these people (his parents) are the whole wide world to him. Long years of growing will slowly move him from the Here and Now to the Then and There.

The two-year-old is not much different. Tell him a story. He dotes on having you simply name his shoes, his shirt, his panties. He loves it when you list what he had for breakfast: milk, orange, cereal. He listens and listens when you tell whom he saw and where he went: mother, daddy, in the car, to the store. The two-year-old lives in a small world, on its main street. His eyes go right a little, left a little, up and down a little, and he has seen all there is to see.

Contrast this with the long view adults can take. Father puts a dollar a week in the Christmas Club so that he can shop forty-eight weeks from now. The college student reads an anatomy book so that he can go to medical school, interne, specialize, and set up practice nine years from now. The man cuts down on cigarettes because he might avoid a cancer forty years from now. The woman takes a vitamin tablet because "it's good for her" even though she feels exactly the same before and after the pill. The adult daydreams about a trip to Hawaii, a land he has only read about. He saves, he plans, he foresees, he prays. A lot of growing has gone on.

Where are your youngsters on this scale? For long years children are hard-headed practical business-

men. They want to see results . . . now. They want
to see what difference it makes to them . . . now.
They are very childish businessmen, of course. They
are not in the market for insurance. They don't care
a whoop about fire protection. They are not going to
buy air-conditioners in the winter time, even though
they are cheaper. They have one concern: What
pays off . . . *now!* And that is the way they have
to be. The growth of their brains, the strength of
their emotional responses, the living they have done
will not let them be any other way.

Even the adolescent gives you a fishy stare and
thinks the cold question: "What do I get out of it?"
Your answer has to be in cold cash passed right over
the counter, not in promissory notes to be paid off in
the future.

The lines of activity and of personalization are not
smooth, even, downward-sloping lines. They have
lumps and bumps in them, some ups and downs.
Adolescents, for example, can be even more self-
centered than nine-year-olds. Adolescents are so
deeply concerned with finding themselves that their
line flares up before it settles down. They are so
aware of their changing bodies, their changing relationships with parents, their changing relationships
with each other. Each day a new self seems to get
out of bed.

Anything which illuminates that self is welcome. They look at literature, at algebra and languages, at history and science, with one big question in mind: "How does this affect *me?*" They mean today's "Me"—the special, different soul who woke up this morning. The person who may someday go to college, or possibly write a lease, or conceivably hold a mortgage is so far off as to be almost unimaginable.

Some More Specific
Suggestions

1. Keep your eye on the youngsters who have been left back. They are sure to be starved for all the success you can feed into them. Don't rub their noses over and over in the weak spots of their past. Do your very best to turn up some way for them to sparkle.

2. At the other end of the spectrum, keep your eyes on your bright children. No one ever feels truly successful when his achievements come with no effort. A person may be pleased to score high; he may feel lucky. But he knows the satisfying sense of having won something only when he works for it.

Be sure that your program makes these intelligent children think and puzzle and dig.

3. Take a second look at anything you are doing in the name of readiness. Some major crimes are committed in that sweet name. A lot of leaf-raking goes on, but we blind ourselves to it by giving it a pretty title. Remember: Growth builds readiness . . . you don't. Good general living builds readiness . . . not workbooks nor paper and pencil and crayons. Be sure that any readiness work you are doing is worthwhile and important *in and of itself*. If it is not the most significant way you can imagine for children to spend their time, drop it. Switch over to the *"Can Do."* Your children will get ready just as soon, and their living will be a thousand times more keen and satisfying.

4. Keep expanding your efforts to individualize what you do. Each year add something new. The primary grades, for example, usually have three groups in reading. But the number three was not handed down from Mt. Sinai. Try having four groups or five or six. And no law limits this approach to the teaching of reading; you can use it in arithmetic, in spelling, in every area you teach. Nor will high school teachers and junior high and upper ele-

mentary staff members get arrested if they try it, too. Small groups work just as well when youngsters are studying Cicero and Caesar as when they study Alice and Jerry. They help people who are struggling with *"p" equals "br"* as much as those who are learning *"nine" take away "six."*

5. Experiment with drill, too. Believe it or not, youngsters love drill. They appreciate it. It makes them feel more competent. But they gag when drill means going over and over stuff they already know or don't give a hoot about. Get more fun out of teaching. See if you can't work out more ways for each child to get the drill he needs. Today too often our dose is geared to that average child who is not there.

Discussion Time

Talk about Interest, and some people get suspicious. They look unhappy. They believe that any medicine will do children more good if it tastes bad. They believe that a wool shirt that scratches will keep the child warmer.

"Whatever They Want to Do Is O.K."

People who react this way are apt to say: "Schools just let children do whatever they like to do."

This accusation is in part true—perfectly true—and it is good to face it: *Children must like what they are doing.* You have no other sure way of knowing that they have grown enough. If youngsters like their work, seek it, and want it, then you can be positive that their whole development has reached the point where they can learn.

But this does not mean that *teachers* are not needed in the classroom. Children must like what they are doing . . . but in school, children must be doing the most significant things they possibly can do. The teacher comes in right here.

The accusation seems to say: Settle for anything that keeps the children happy. This is completely false. This is not a school's job. No good teacher lets children do *just* what they want to do. The youngsters must want to do it, yes. But what they do—the "it"—must be the best they are capable of . . . the most important learning they can be doing . . . that which will contribute the most. A school is **not** a movie house; it is not a circus; it is not party time. A teacher's job is not to put on a show or to entertain. School is where children go to learn. They won't learn unless they like their work, but unless they learn, it is not school.

A teacher's first job is to know: What are the significant facts in life? What counts? What matters? What makes a difference to our country and our world? What changes the way people live? What adds to human happiness and what ends misery?

A teacher—nursery school, first grade, high school —is a student of society. A teacher is a student of children.

A teacher—nursery school, first grade, high school —is a scholar and a specialist in knowledge. A teacher is an expert on children.

The two must go together. Children and facts. Children and ideas. Children and significant behavior. Children and key attitudes. The child must like what he is doing, but what he does in school can never be lollypops or whipped cream, fluff, the frosting on the cake. The child—eagerly, happily, wanting to—must be sinking his teeth into the crucial facts or skills or attitudes of life. He must be meeting the ideas that will make a difference to him and to the society of which he is a part.

This is the teacher's job. The child likes what he is doing, *and* what he is doing is important. From all the million and one things that a child has grown enough to do, the teacher helps him focus on the best.

"*You Can Do It in Sports, but . . .*"

A great many head-shakers say that it is easy enough to get enthusiasm from youngsters in sports and games. They claim it is almost impossible in the academic areas. When you come right down to it, isn't history a little dull compared to football, or reading drab when you stack it against Run, Sheep, Run? The question is: Don't you have to make children learn whether they want to or not?

Of course most youngsters do love sports. But to say that sports and games are all that children love undersells the human.

We humans have distinctive characteristics that mark us off from other animals. We can talk. We can do much more intricate thinking. We can analyze. We can generalize. We can look ahead and foresee. We are capable of coping with abstract ideas.

We can remember more. Sum it up: We are smarter than four-legged animals; we have more brain power.

In every area of life people want to use their power. They want to function up to their peak. They want to make the most of what they have. Why should not this strong drive operate in the intellectual realm as well? The intellectual realm is our distinctive bailiwick. The fact is that humans particularly want to function well here.

There is much evidence to back up this fact. Take five-year-olds, for example. Is their idea of heaven to run and shout, to climb and make believe? Yes. But a five-year-old's heaven is a big place. He is fascinated by a story of how children are adopted. He sits enthralled when you tell him why a sick person's stomach must be pumped. He is enchanted by a tale about a snake losing its skin. A five-year-old is muscle and movement *and* mind, too.

Every age is. Children have a burning curiosity. They are sponges, soaking up knowledge. They are pests, plying you with questions. They are big ears, listening to conversations that were never meant for them. They are specialists in the third degree, probing and poking until they find out what they want to know.

Youngsters love activity. They thrive on the social relations that go along with games. They want to test themselves out; sports offer a chance to do this. But the human is a rounded creature. Dogs, cows, sheep, worms may be one-track . . . but not people. All of us can get excited about an idea.

We do differ, of course. Some children are more book-minded than others. Some more academically skilled. Some much better organized intellectually than others. And some boys and girls have better coordinated bodies and stronger urges to use their bodies.

Despite the range, if a child has enough intellectual ability to be in a school and not in an institution, there are facts he will want to learn. There are ideas he will respond to. There are subjects—history, science, mathematics, literature—that will be useful to him.

You can say: "Children don't want to use their brains." From the standpoint of Child Development such a statement denies the very nature of man. Or you can say: "The trick is in finding out how to reach each child" . . . and that looks like the more valid and ethical way of stating the problem.

"But with 35 in a Class!"

This latter way makes sense to a lot of people but they cannot see a practical answer. They look at their class size and come up with: "It's all right in theory but . . . just as a practical matter, don't you have to make some children study, whether they want to or not, whether the particular study interests them or not?"

This is quite a question. There is no getting away from it: Teaching thirty-five in a class is one of the hardest jobs in the world. The strain on a teacher's strength, the demands on a teacher's imagination and ingenuity, are enormous. The public simply does not realize what the teaching job is today.

But you have to make a decision for yourself. What are you going to believe? In what direction are you going to bend your efforts? You can let pressures on you force you into accepting bad theory: Children are all the same. . . . They can learn anything at any time if you put enough heat on them. . . . It doesn't make any real difference to people if they feel good about life or not. Or you can cling to sound theory. You can do your best under the circumstances you face. You can work for improved conditions so that someday you can operate on a theory that makes sense to you.

In the long run money is the answer to these pressures: money for buildings, money for teachers, money to reduce class size. If you want a partial answer for the immediate present, here is one suggestion: Call in your parents. Draft them. Bring them into your classroom. Turn them into assistant teachers. Make teacher-aides out of them. Every single day have two or three or four parents working right beside you, teaching in the classroom with you.

Schools and children and teachers need a revolutionary approach right now. We need a device immediately to insure that every child can find some intellectual content that he can master and put to good use. Drafting the help of parents is the only solution that will overnight let the boys and girls in school today have the teacher-pupil ratio that decent education demands.[1]

"*You Will Make Them Soft*"

Practicalities are a stumbling block. But even in assuming something can be done, if you keep search-

[1] This idea is developed further in James L. Hymes, Jr., *Effective Home-School Relations* (New York: Prentice-Hall, Inc., 1953).

ing for children's interests, don't you make children soft? How will they ever learn that life is not a bed of roses? After all, no one of us is head-over-heels in love with all of his work.

This much can be said straight out: Any approach that makes children "soft" is bad. Unless all signs fail, our country has hard times ahead of it. We may face war. We certainly face problems. The 1970's, 1980's, when these youngsters will be grown up, surely will demand sacrifices, toughness, a realistic ability to do whatever-job-is-there-and-has-to-be-done.

But you build strength when you work with children. You weaken youngsters when you work against them.

The more mature a person is, the more able he is to cope with the unpleasant. The less mature the human is, the more he must have everything his own way and the easy way. The two-year-old cries when he is crossed; the three-year-old gives up in disgust when the going is rough. But year after year, if children develop healthfully, their capacity to face up to reality deepens.

When you treat children with friendliness, when you help them find success, you foster this normal, natural unfolding. The youngster who is ill-treated

is the bad bet. He grows . . . in size. He grows . . .
in years. But his feelings, unsatisfied, remain those of
a two-year-old or a Three.

No end of evidence supports this point of view.
The most convincing comes from our wars. Fighting
men are under terrific stress. Each man has his own
individual breaking point, but those who best take
the rigors of war are the ones with good childhoods
in back of them. Those who crumble easiest are the
ones life has hurt: men with not enough good experiences with parents, with teachers, with friends.
You need never fear that the child whose needs have
been met will be the weakling. Your good living with
him helps make him a tower of strength.

Actually we can all see evidence about interest
with our own eyes that ought to give convincing
answers. When a child is interested he works his
head off. He gives the job everything he has. His
interest carries him over the rough spots and the
dirty work—the tough and hard parts of the job. He
takes these in his stride and thinks nothing of them.
Interest does not make children soft. It is the secret
ingredient that makes them work like beavers.

The youngsters are putting on a play? They paint
floors, hammer a set together, scrub the seats to make
them clean, memorize their lines. Their interest is

exclusively in the performance, but they do all the nasty jobs too without a second thought.

The youngsters are running their own store? They drill on arithmetic so they can make change, they struggle to make the handwriting on their signs clear, they practice until their reading is down pat. The real fun comes from working in the store but these other jobs, which call for accuracy and care and correctness, are tied in inescapably with their interest. Youngsters accept them.

When a child's reason for working is some external reward, or the fear of some imposed punishment, you have to be on your toes. Then children will take the easy way out. They will do as little as possible just so long as they get the reward or escape the punishment. Then children will shirk if they can get away with it, or loaf or escape. You breed cheating.

But if youngsters have their hearts set on painting their classroom, they can't cheat on stirring the paint. They can't skip painting behind the doors, hoping that no one will remember to look there. Painting the room is their idea, their project, their plan. They can't fool themselves. They have nothing to get out of. If you want youngsters to live a rigorous life because you think they need the practice for what lies ahead, working through their interests is the path for you.

And the important point is: Youngsters enjoy being eager beavers. Blood, sweat and tears are their meat. When they put themselves into a job—into the scrubbing *and* the glory—children have a glow. They may gripe along the way. Some ages do, and some ages go in for exaggerated exasperation and complaints. They may want a lot of "coffee breaks"; younger children in particular must have their hard-work periods carefully timed. But the solid satisfaction in achievement, in learning, in mastery tastes very good indeed to growing youngsters.

You have to keep searching for children's interests. Once you find them, don't let the youngsters off easy. They don't want you to. They want you to have high standards, just as long as the learning makes sense to them. They want you to hold them to the grindstone, and they respect you and are grateful when you do. They want your expectations to stretch them up to the peak of their growing powers. They count on you to ask the most searching questions, to check them on details, to open up the next step in thinking or doing. Youngsters want to achieve.

4

Your Youngsters Must Like Themselves

*Y*our children like you. They like their work. You have really made headway. These two good states feed right into the next Child Development suggestion: *Your youngsters must like themselves.*

The way you live with your youngsters must build in them a wonderful Tarzan feeling: a surge of their own strength, of their own importance. You want them to beat their chests proudly and to let out a whoop of joy. They are glad they are who they are.

101

They are glad they are as big as they are because of all they now know and all they can now do.

The Child Development Background

The human is a rocket ship, intended to be airborne, to head upward and outward with a rush. A youngster needs only one year or so of living, then he has his basic tools—just the first year of his life and then he is off. By that time he has upright posture: He can stand, he can see; the world begins to be his oyster. He has forward locomotion: He can move and go and be on his own. His arms and his hands and his fingers are starting to do what he wants them to do, the world is coming within reach. And the child can talk. What more do you need for a start to be a person?

From that point on in a million ways, through everything they do, children show us how much they want to be big. Ask a youngster to help you gather some firewood. Twigs are not for him. He tries to lug the log you can barely lift. Did you forget the key to your house? Ask the children for help. The whole neighborhood will volunteer to climb in through the

window. You are painting your house? Your child-
helpers will be glad to do the roof for you; they want
to perch on top of the ladder or swing with one arm
from the drain pipe or dormer.

Youngsters always have their eyes on the big job,
the hard one. Once any task is mastered and routine,
it loses its allure; it no longer serves the child's pur-
pose although you still may want the job done. The
three-year-old loves to wash your dishes; not the ten-
year-old, thank you. The five-year-old loves to wash
your windows; not the twelve-year-old, thank you.
The Four will vacuum rugs that do not need clean-
ing; the fourteen-year-old is too tired even to push
the button.

Youngsters always relish the unusual. Whatever
opens up a new world to them—a world in which
they can be bigger and bigger people—is clearly their
favorite. An upper bunk has it all over the lower
bunk—who wants to stay close to the ground? Riding on the running board is a thousand times more
appealing than sitting on the staid old seat. Going
out of doors after dark simply is not in the same
league with going out in daytime; one gives you a
very special feeling while the other is humdrum.

For the same reason, whatever defies the usual
laws is the child's special dish. Where are people

supposed to sleep? In a bed, of course, so youngsters love sleeping on the floor, sleeping in a hammock, sleeping out-of-doors, or not sleeping at all. At one age staying up until midnight is a thrill; at a later age daybreak becomes the goal (even if they can hardly keep their eyes open). Where are people supposed to be? On the ground, of course, out in the open in standard upright fashion. Young children's greatest fun comes when they are under tables or under chairs or under anything. Older youngsters are in seventh heaven if they have a tree house. Playing in a cave is a joy for any age. Youngsters think they are little when they have to do things the ordinary way.

Their goal is to be in the driver's seat. They are pleased with anything they can steer, with any motor that makes a noise. Watch a three-year-old on his tricycle; he has power and he loves it. Watch the four-year-old. He sits behind the steering wheel of a parked car, turns the wheel, pretends to drive. He is in a delightful dream world. Watch Fives at play. They ride horses, fly planes, speed in boats and cars and trucks . . . and they make all the noises that go with force and strength.

Small wonder that merry-go-rounds are so popular. The small fry feel that they are going so fast and riding so high. That is the way they like to feel. Older boys and girls have their hearts set on a real horse, on a real scooter, on a motorcycle. All ages want the same sensation.

Young children are very direct. Their play reveals clearly what they prize. You see these youngsters all dressed up in cowboy gear: holsters, spurs, belts, hats. When a cowboy shoots, he is big. The "bang-bang" means the child has power, and that is what he wants. Of course cowboys are kid stuff, and space men are for the little ones. But another age wants a BB gun, and still another a .22.

From the very beginning real thrills come when a child does something by himself. He is Two, and he blows out a match! His whole face is wreathed in smiles. He is Three, and he builds a tower of blocks! He grins from ear to ear. He is Four, and he puts his own fare in the case box of the bus! The buttons almost pop off his coat. He is Five, and you let him turn the ignition key in the automobile! The child hardly rides in the car; he sails through the air.

Under six or over sixteen, all ages lobby continuously for their rights. They plead their case everlastingly: "I am *so* old enough . . ." to stay up until eight . . . to go to the movies alone . . . to ride my bicycle in the street . . . to have a real

football uniform . . . to drink coffee . . . to use
lipstick and to date. Children are very touchy. They
instantly spot and shake off anything that types them
as young or small or dependent. The three-year-old
does not want you to hold his hand when you cross
the street. The ten-year-old walks behind you or in
front of you but not by your side; someone might
think he was your "child."

Every age fights for itself in its own way. The
young child uses his play to make himself feel big.
Preadolescents put on a great show of bravado:
noise, wisecracks, flip remarks. They want the world
to know that they are not little children any more,
nice and good and sweet and well-behaved.

Adolescents take our breath away with their sharp
opinions, their flat and definite stands on what they
like and what they hate. Everyone within earshot
must understand that they have ideas and tastes of
their own. If you want to predict what their opinions
will be look at your own and choose the opposite.
Your batting average will be remarkably good. This
age has to stand over there, clear and out in the
open, so you will notice them.

Preadolescents and adolescents seem like utter
conformists. Their dress, their language, their pas-
sions, and their raves are carbon copies. But the

carbon paper is always pressed against their own age, not our old age. These older boys and girls are leaning, but they are not leaning on us. Look quickly and you may think that they are not standing on their own two feet at all. But listen! Underneath there is almost a "yah-yah-yah." They are saying: "We are not tied to you. We have found our pals."

No child who is in school wants to think of himself as a dependent little person. Every child want to have a decent respect for himself. He wants to be big. He wants to be powerful. He wants to be *somebody*. He must have a picture in his mind of himself as a growing person. The picture must be a real one —not some Napoleonic super-rosy daydream. But the real picture must be a satisfying one. He must be glad he is as big as he is because of all he can now do.

Your school task is to capitalize on this desire. You get an A if your youngsters go home at the end of a day boasting: "Do you know what *we* saw . . . Do you know where *we* went . . . Do you know what *we* did?" You can feel content because your children will. But if they complain, "They treat us like babies," beware.

Some Special Social Conditions

Little children—preschoolers still at home—get a lot of backing in their urge to grow. In America we like independent little fellows. We admire gumption and an up-and-at-them quality. We are all for independence. We are glad to feed children—little children—a diet that strengthens their sense of themselves.

We have invented blue-jean training pants. Even tiny tots can scoot about, crawling and hunching and getting where they want to go. No "mama-babies" for us. We are pleased when a little one takes off. That is the sign we like to see.

We don't put long dresses on our babies. We don't bind their feet—we don't even put shoes on them. The well-dressed two-year-old is in overalls. He is free to stretch and climb and amble. The well-dressed five-year-old has no ruffles, no pleats, no patent leather. Boy or girl, the Five is in jeans, free to run and dig.

We put zippers and buttons children can manage in their clothes. We are saying, "You can do it."

We put steps in front of the toilet. "You can

reach." We find spoons children can grip, glasses they can hold, pitchers they can pour from.

From an early age we give youngsters an allowance. "This is your money; spend it as you wish."

We buy toys galore, from crib days on. Not one of them says: Be passive, be accepting. The dumbbell rattle for the baby shouts: Shake me, I make a noise . . . Bite me, I'm washable. The hammer bed for the two-year-old says: Hit me, you're strong . . . Hit me again. The Three has his wheelbarrow, the Four his wagon. All these younger ages have blocks and clay and paint. They have shovels to dig with. We give our children toy irons, toy mops, toy washing machines, toy soda fountains, fire engines, tractors, cash registers. We din into their ears for a while: "You are big . . . you are almost as big as mother and father."

We listen when children talk, as if they really were people.

We give them reasons when we talk, just as if they were human.

We try to take their preferences into account. Even when the children are very small we pay attention to what they like to eat and wear, what stories they enjoy hearing, where they prefer to go, and what playmates they like to see. In this country you

don't have to be twenty-one to vote . . . in families.
Children cast their votes from eighteen *months* on,
and their vote is counted, too.

A *"Reducing Diet"*

The hunger for independence is inside of children,
normal and natural. We whet their appetites and
make the desire more keen. Then, as youngsters
move on out of homes, we put them on a "reducing
diet."

Our way of living today cuts children down to size.
At the very time when boys and girls are looking for
more and more nourishment our modern, mechanical, technical world starts giving them a meagre
meal.

In days gone by a six-year-old could ride a horse.
Today a youngster has to be sixteen to drive a car.
Once an eight-year-old could work right along beside his father. He could hand Dad a tool or hold
the wood straight. Today father is in a factory at the
edge of town or in an office in the busy center—no
children allowed. Once a youngster could split the
firewood. Today families turn a switch for heat, but

they will get the child a Boy Scout knife when he is ten . . . if he proves he can be careful.

Once youngsters had to bring in the cows. This was a nasty job, but it was a job. It gave a child the sense that he was big when he did it. Today he lives in an apartment house. The "animals" he cares for are his turtle, or perhaps a parakeet. Life is big; children are made to feel small. They can ride their bikes, but not in the street and not on the sidewalk. They can sleep out overnight but only in a pup tent on the back lawn.

The possessions in most homes are expensive. "Don't fool with the TV; you will break it." "Don't fiddle with your watch; it is a good one." "Keep your hands off the hi-fi." Our houses are cluttered with things, and the things are too precious for experimentation.

The things are complex too. A child could mow the lawn—one age really wants to!—but the family has a power mower, and the job is too dangerous. Even adults do not know what makes our intricate machines tick: "I can tell you which key starts the car but if anything goes wrong, I'm lost. I call a mechanic."

Specialists take over. Youngsters have a hard time getting their foot in the door. Bread is baked . . .

somewhere. Clothes sewn . . . somewhere. Cows are milked . . . somewhere. Laws are made and problems are solved by somebody . . . somewhere.

Life is handed to children readymade. Youngsters have a hard time establishing their own identity and leaving their own mark on the world around them as they grow up. They can buy their Christmas cards or Valentines two for five cents at the dime store. The cards are all printed—just sign your name. They can buy a leather kit. The pieces are all cut out— just sew them together. They can buy a woodburning set. The wood is all marked—just follow the lines. Finished products look fine, but how does the child seem inside? Does he feel good? Is he truly proud?

School: A Workshop

School can be a natural corrective to much of this. The simple act of going to school makes a youngster feel big. He is out of his home, away on his own. He cannot hear his parents' worrying ideas. He is one in a crowd, not the only one with mother watching everything he does. He has the chance to escape some of the familiar "don'ts" and "mustn'ts" that he has heard for years. School is a different setting. The youngster stands on his own two feet. The reminders of babyhood are at home, locked in a closet.

The whole stage is set. We promote youngsters year after year: private, corporal, sergeant, lieutenant . . . on up to four-star general (which may be eighth grade or twelfth). Our whole system is geared to making a fellow puff out and out, with each new step ahead.

School can mean that a child does things. Last year he couldn't, but this year he can. Last year he was too young or he did not know enough, but this year he can. Knowledge is power, and that is what children want. Skills and facts give know-how, and children want that. The more they know, the more they can do, the more able they are, the more contentment grows inside.

But not any old school can turn the trick. You have to keep in mind: Once young men and young women married when they were sixteen. Today Sixteen is just a boy or a girl, a junior in high school. Many a young adolescent looks at a page of algebra and moans: "I'll be dead before I ever do anything." $2x^2 - 5xy - 7y^2$ is not a very vigorous life for a red-blooded growing human.

Schools today have some very fast competition. A child must sit—nine to three, September to June—but he can always dream. His body may be nailed down fast to a chair and a desk the way a baby is locked in a high chair. But his mind can wander. He can have a part-time self. That little part of him can fuss with gerunds and with participles, with two-fish-plus-four-fish-are-how-many-fish-and-then-color-them-purple. Rivals can capture children's full minds and attention and energies.

The screen magazines can "take" these young people to Hollywood. The pops records can "take" them to Broadway. The comics can "take" them to outer space. Radio can "transport" them to the frozen Yukon or to the heart of the steaming jungle. Television and the movies offer fabulous tinsel adventures. Life need not stay drab and childish.

Today boys and girls have unusual invitations to dream. But children are not escapists by nature. They are not shirkers, loafers, or floaters. They want their real life to have significance. They want to find in reality the proof of their own importance, the proof of their own real power. Will they feel big in your school, or must they turn to cardboard and sham?

You, in Your Classroom

Youngsters catch your attitude. They are very sensitive to how you feel about them and to what goes on in your mind. Deep down in your marrow you have to feel sure that your boys and girls are big people.

Everyone shows his good feelings in a different way. But two points are clear for everyone: You cannot get by with honeyed words: "My! How big you all are." And you cannot use good words as a club: "I should think that big people like you would certainly know better than that!" You must feel, deep down inside yourself, that you face growing striving youngsters . . . real people . . . not to be pushed around. Respect them, and they will respect themselves.

Parents often find it hard to give children credit for all the growing they have done. Mothers and fathers are so close to their youngsters. Growth creeps up on parents day by day. The child is six and all set for first grade; his parents still think of him as "Junior" or "Baby" or "Sonny." The girl is fourteen, mature physically, and very ready for high school; her parents still think of her as "Sis" . . . the little one. Only yesterday parents were changing diapers, feeding the child, making all the decisions. Even when a man is fully grown, with a family of his own, his mother—living with him or visiting—may automatically remind him in the morning: "Don't forget your handkerchief."

You may face a similar problem. Year after year you see fourth-graders or ninth-graders. You become very aware of all their weaknesses and foibles. You come to feel very responsible and necessary. When you stay with one age for any length of time your impression is: "How young they are . . . how small . . . how immature."

I once was director of a camp for boys nine to twelve years of age. One summer we decided to lower our age range to include eight-year-olds. They were our "babies." We felt very daring to include children so young, and we made careful plans to protect them. The following fall I worked in a nursery school for two to five-year-olds. In that setting the five-year-olds seemed so big, so capable, so very grown up. In comparison with the two-year-olds in the school the Fives looked huge, as if they could cope with anything that came along.

Here is one good recommendation: Each September, before school starts, take a long look at a newborn baby! No matter what age you teach, your youngsters will seem big when you meet them. (Maybe you should take a spoonful of this medicine once every month. Call it your "prescription for perspective.")

If your youngsters look real and human and growing to you the chances are that you will talk to them: man-to-man, face-to-face, looking them straight in the eye. You won't always be "teacher"— the child looking up, you looking down. The chances are that you will joke with them: good fun, some real laughs. You won't always be "teacher"— the child attentive, and you earnest. The chances are that you will listen to them: the boys and girls talking and you the interested one. You won't always be "teacher"—the child reciting, and you grading. You will have some conversation.

Flowing from Your Feelings

Impressed with how able your children are, you will have little trouble coming through with other experiences that fit them. Jobs are important to think about. What honest-to-goodness work can your group do? Strange as it sounds, service is children's motto. They love to give it. The more real labor you

get out of your youngsters, the better they like life
and the better they like themselves.

The problem, as always, is to hit your children
right smack in the middle. If the job is too far beyond or too far below them, they feel imposed upon.
We all know that some youngsters will give anything
to be on Safety Patrol. Older children have to be
dragooned; they look on the work as baby stuff.

Jobs must be graded the way textbooks are. And
there must be a continuous never-ending supply of
them, right on through high school. When children
are young their responsibilities will probably be in
their classroom. But very soon that becomes too
"homey." Youngsters want to make contributions to
the school as a whole. And before long you have to
find ways for boys and girls to give service to their
communities. You need simple short-duration tasks
at first, longer and more continuing responsibilities
as the grades go along.

You and your colleagues can go over every part of
your school with a fine-tooth comb. Whenever you
come across a job that an adult is doing, ask yourself: Could a child do this? Whenever you find a job
that is not being done—something you wish some
adult would do—ask yourself: Could a child do this?
Look at everyone who is working: the secretary, the

mailman, the gardener, the carpenter, plumber, painter, switchboard operator, motion picture operator, the mimeographer. Ask yourself: Could a child do the work?

In the primary grades boys and girls water plants and feed the fish. This is standard stuff. It is fine for five-year-olds! Sixes, Sevens, Eights need more to sink their teeth into. Twelves need more, and Fifteens still more. School is a child's world. Its sanitation can be his problem. Its welfare. Its food. Its recreation. Its upkeep and health and management. We have to learn to look for work opportunities in more places than our classrooms. Schools also have boiler rooms and store rooms, lunch rooms and offices, hallways and sidewalks, libraries, stages, closets.

Unusual, spectacular settings—Boys' Towns and European refugee communities—turn the whole business of living and maintenance over to young people. Hold a similar goal for your school. Make your school the place in the community where boys and girls do everything—up to the limits of their abilities.

When you have exhausted the work possibilities in school, be sure that you have exhausted the children before you stop looking. Your boys and girls have abilities that your towns can use. Their hands and brains are aching to go to work. Give your locality a microscopic examination. What needs doing? If your community makes your youngsters sit on their hands because they are in school, it is not doing children a favor. Save the unemployment for the very young or the super-aged.

The Bigness of Life

Trips are another educational device that can give youngsters a true sense of growing. Children who spend all their time within the four walls of a school feel cooped in. Travel is in the spirit of our times: to go places, to see things. When your youngsters take a school trip some of the bigness of life rubs off on them.

These trips, of course, are not a mere change of scenery or a chance for some gulps of fresh air. No matter what you teach, somewhere in your community someone is using your subject matter and applying it to life's problems. Maybe your boys and girls can see a newspaper reporter or a sports writer or advertising copy man struggle with the English language. Or they can watch farm produce come in at the freight yards. They can talk with a judge or a jailer or see a jury or a junkman. Let them, and a change takes place. Subject matter no longer is a mire they are stuck in because they are little and must still go to school. Youngsters begin to see facts and knowledge and skills as the stuff of life itself.

Fifth grade (or any grade) must never be a pen that a child is trapped in because he is small and cannot get out to see life by himself. Our slogan has to be: "Join the school and see the world." We do take young children on little trips. Now we have to make the logical and psychological extension of this good idea: Take bigger children on bigger trips, on more of them, and let the youngsters be more independent.

One possibility is to make more use of parents. A committee of five students with one parent to guide them can cover a lot of territory in a town. And in some communities there are even trips that older students can make on their own. We cannot continue to say to growing boys and girls: Because you are older you must stay closer to school. Each year our theme must be: *Because you are so big* you must see more and more of life.

If you think well of trips you can also make use of

the first cousin of the field trip: bringing people into your classroom. This is the easiest of all devices to handle and one of the most gratifying. Everyone has a good time. The visitor is thrilled and the youngsters get a feeling of pride: "Do you know whom we met today?" That boasting—about the school because the school makes the children feel important—is what you want to hear from your students.

Visitors are old hat in the lower grades. The primary years have a parade of policemen, firemen, milkmen, and farmers. But older youngsters need a longer parade, with many more participants. Simply going to school is almost thrill enough when a child is very small. We have to step up our offerings as these children step up.

Who comes? It depends on what you are studying. But a city detective will be glad to come. The trainer for the local ball team. A transcontinental truck driver. A feature story writer on your daily paper. The brakeman on a train. The people, both sexes, who make a town or city tick, who do its work and who know its life . . . they will all be glad to come. And a youngster will be proud that he is in eighth grade. If he were not so big these wonderful things would not happen.

Facts, Skills, and Know-How

Of course you do not have to be spectacular every day. The regular work of the school also feeds right in to children's urge to grow. Facts are a child's best friend. Skills have a Number One priority. The more children know, the bigger they feel.

But use all your imagination and all your flair.

Youngsters want to show off with some of their learning. They want to be able to hold an audience with it. They want to command attention. For them some learning has to be like a parlor trick: People will look and stare and be amazed.

Two and two is four? Everyone knows that.

Capitalize the first word of a sentence? Everyone knows that.

A youngster searching to find his own special self —all children are!—wants to know something that will make him stand out. If all the learning is run-of-the-mill stuff, he has no special possession, and he is not special either.

It will pay to ask yourself: What did my class do today that they could talk about? Run a power jig-saw? Learn to read a timetable? Fix the washer in a leaky faucet? Make a doorbell for the classroom with **dry cell batteries**? Look through a microscope? Hold a snake? Construct a filter for the aquarium? Use a brace and bit? Read a barometer?

Check to be sure that through the days you are giving them some conversation pieces. Your goal is to teach them something they could not possibly have known if they had not come to school. Then school becomes a useful place in their eyes: It is the place they go to feel bigger.

The People's Choice

They will feel bigger, too, if they have a real voice in the running of their school. No matter how democratic families try to be, many decisions at home are made for children: what they will eat, when they go to bed, where they can go. Running a family democratically is complicated. The age span is so great, from grandmother down to the infant. So many issues are subtle, involving what the boss wants, what the neighbors think, what the budget will stand. Adolescents speak their minds about this state of affairs. You often hear them say: "I'm just a slave" . . . "It's taxation without representation" . . . "This is worse than communism; they are always telling you what to do."

School is the child's particular world. This is where he can speak out and be heard. A youngster senses this. In his eyes a claim has been filed. This spot of land is for boys and girls. Relatives, babies, bosses—all are poachers here. Stakes mark the spot: School is for children.

Here, if children feel that ideas are rammed down their throats, they feel doubly small. They do not like it, and they are crushed. But here, when their ideas count, they feel big. They do like that, and they are for you. The more you expand the areas where youngsters have a voice, the more good you do for children, and the more good you do for yourself.

If you give youngsters the chance to decide, of course you have to stick by their decisions. You cannot go along with them when the decision is agreeable but veto it anytime you disagree. Nor can you get by with giving them loaded choices: "Do you want arsenic or would you prefer to be shot?" Youngsters get their sense of bigness from true citizenship, not from the outward signs of it.

If you are hesitant about opening up too many matters to children's choice, start by getting their opinion. Make it clear that you are not asking for a vote. You want their advice, their reactions, and suggestions. If children know you mean this seriously, they will respond. You give yourself a chance to test out their capacities, and to gear yourself to them as you go along.

Some More Specific Suggestions

1. In our Western part of the world we all seem to believe that Orientals hate to lose face. This may or may not be true of our Far Eastern friends, but it is very true of children. Beware of anything that embarrasses youngsters or publicly pulls them down. If you have to talk with a child, do it face to face. In private. Keep your dissatisfaction or disapproval a confidential matter, something just between the two of you. It is hard to know how the Puritan felt when he was in the stocks, exposed to public scorn, but it is not hard to know what a child thinks. No youngster can take shame or sarcasm or having his weaknesses hung out on the line.

2. Watch out for type-casting. It is easy to put a youngster in a role and expect him to play it. This is the villain . . . the heavy . . . the bad man with the black horse and the mustache. A child wants a

good picture of himself; but he must have some picture, good or bad. If we insist, he will settle for the villain's role and live up to it. He will invite us to cast him as that type again and again. Be sure each of your youngsters has some chance to play the lover and the hero.

3. The people to watch out for most of all are your failures: the youngsters who have been left back, the boys and girls who get low C's or who slide by with 66 or 64. A school cannot go along playing the same music to these children year after year: If you don't succeed we will fail you . . . If you don't succeed we will tell your parents . . . If you don't succeed we will keep you in. These youngsters need some individual help. Why are they not learning? What is their specific trouble? What strengths do they have? Talk to these boys and girls. Get at their particular misconceptions and misunderstandings. No child who fails time after time can think well of himself. With individual work you can save many of these youngsters from a black and murky look.

4. Keep your eye on your quiet children, too. Some of these youngsters are happy; they simply do not make a lot of noise. But many of your shy children would love to star a bit. You cannot push them to the forefront—they will shrink back. You cannot

force them into prominence—they will shrivel up. But you may be able subtly to grease some ways so that occasionally these youngsters slide into being the "big shot." You will do their souls a lot of good.

Discussion Time

Very few people object to the general notion of helping youngsters feel good about themselves. Once you break this down into specifics, however, doubts arise. In schools questions about failure immediately come to the fore. Many people favor failure. They are persuaded that an occasional failure makes youngsters learn to "take it." They want children to learn that they cannot get by with no effort at all.

"Should Children Never Fail?"

Actually there is no point in arguing against failure—that would be like objecting to day and night, or opposing the sun. A child cannot live without experiencing failure. Failure is a part of his life everywhere around him.

A common adult pastime is to become nostalgic about childhood. We do this particularly when our own feet hurt and when we have shooting pains in our poor aching backs. Then childhood looks like such a happy carefree cheerful time. We forget all of its torturous moments, and childhood has many of them.

Youngsters fail time and time again. They fail simply because they are small or weak or light or not coordinated enough or because they cannot think well enough. Youngsters fail because their age-mates are harder on them than we ever would be. Youngsters fail because their hopes and aspirations are beyond them. They fail tens of times in a day, just as naturally and inevitably as breathing.

The baby is struggling to walk, and he falls. The ten-year-old is dying to hit the ball, and he hits only fouls. The fifteen-year-old is living in anguish, hoping that this time she will be asked to the dance. A little realism will tell us that children are well acquainted with failure. We do not have to think up ways to fail them in order to stiffen their back bones. We do not have to serve extra helpings of failure simply to remind youngsters that there is such a thing.

Boys and girls get such full doses of failure, just as

they live their normal lives, that we must be very cautious about any man-imposed trouble. One thing you can be sure of: The child who has known too much failure is a weak child. His spirit is bound to be undermined.

Some schools, casually and almost as a matter of routine, fail a certain number of children in every grade. This is like divorce. Yet these schools forcibly separate children from their friends and their age-mates as an everyday matter. Actually this is worse than divorce. The child is left with nothing but a blacker, dimmer, gloomier picture of himself.

Somehow we in school work must learn to understand that failure is a sharp hurting knife if used on a school-age child. If we must use it, we can at least regard it with the awe and respect the surgeon shows for his scalpel. The school that wields failure like a meat axe makes mincemeat of children's attitudes toward themselves.

This note of caution does not imply that continuous promotion solves everything. Many wise schools have no failure in their first three grades. Considering the varying rates at which children grow, this is simple, good sense. More schools should do it. Considering the blow that failure is for a child, more schools should do it at all age levels—not just the primary grades. But we need a string constantly around our fingers: Promoting the child who has not learned is only the first step.

A school must galvanize into action to find out why the child didn't learn in the first place. Promotion is only a technique, an arrangement. In and of itself, it does not solve any problems.

A child wants success. He wants a feeling of honest accomplishment. He has to know that there are important things he can do. Promote him, yes! But plan for him, and plan with him. A child does not learn just because he is put ahead, any more than he learns simply because he is left behind. The teaching job is still there to do. Confront that child with facts he can learn! Help him feel good about himself.

"Children Have Too Much Power as It Is"

Some adults think that children feel too good about themselves. They think that youngsters today have too much power. They want to see more homes and schools where youngsters know their place and stay in it.

Some boys and girls in your class may make even

you feel this way . . . and very strongly. But before you make up your mind, ask yourself: "Are these particular children sick or are they well?"

Often the youngsters who want power so much that you can hardly live with them are troubled children. They have been hurt, and they are the exceptions. Beware about generalizing to all children from the few who have very special needs.

Healthy school-agers will relish every legitimate chance you give them to do a job, to be on their own, to carry a responsibility, to make a contribution, but most school children are not starved for such chances. They do not have to grab for them.

Developmentally, two-year-olds do. They want their own way. They assert themselves. A million and one times they have to prove how important they are. Threes are power-seekers. Four-year-olds are. This is what the preschool years are for: They are the time when a youngster can throw his weight around a bit and find himself. But then he has himself. Each year, if a youngster gets a break, and if people take him seriously, a child can take himself more for granted. He has made his point.

Somehow these few children who seem too big for their britches have been cheated. Actually, they have not had enough chances to be big. Now they are almost ready to explode. Their normal, natural drive for importance has been so blocked, and for so long, that at this point power is all they can think of. Maybe their parents believed that little children should be seen but not heard. Maybe some other member of the family gets all the glory and, at home, these children get only the leavings. Sometimes a child who has a history of illness, who has had to be restrained, acts this way. A child who never had enough love and attention can act too big and too wise and too all-important. There can be all kinds of causes.

You do see these youngsters in schools. They can be all ages, but they act like two-year-olds. Don't let these exceptions blind you to the way eight-year-olds can act, or twelve-year-olds, or sixteens. These older ages all want independence, but they can be sensible about it. If they are in balance they do not have to go off the deep end; they need not grasp for something that has become overly precious.

"Do We Really Want These Drives in Our Children?"

The words Bigness and Power have a nasty sound. They call to mind memories of Hitler and of the

Russians. Some people wonder: Is this what we want for our children?

Keep in mind that the person to beware of is the one who has never had enough, whose need is still sky-high. He stays power-driven. He is the menace, not the one who has had some decent sense of his own importance as he has grown up.

The need to be big is so important that it does not go away just because it is not met. It is not a luxury or an added extra fillip in life, something a person can have or do without. The human is so made that he must get a full sense of his own importance. The human has no choice. If he does not get it one way he will get it another. If he does not get it at one time he will get it at another. But in order to live— power is just like food, air, sleep—the human must feel that he is important.

When a youngster gets this awareness of himself at home and in school he is a good bet. You can count on him as the years go along. He won't have to push people around. He won't have to be overly bossy. He won't always have to be on top or always get his way. Such a person has a good feeling about himself. He does not have to go all through life trying to prove that he is somebody. When you help your youngsters to feel big you help keep them in balance.

"Will They Ever Stop Once They Start?"

This idea is hard for many people to believe. It goes against all we know about habits. Teachers wonder: If Power and Bigness are so good tasting won't youngsters seek more and more, on without end?

Don't forget: We are people, not mechanical rabbits who must always run in the same groove. We are not pegged. We grow, we change, we develop. Child Development keeps saying this over and over and over.

Look at six-year-olds. They always have to come in first; losing almost kills them. Yet the very same youngsters at ten are super good sports. They feel like heroes when they say: "We lost, but it was a good game."

Or look at the games six-year-olds play. Their activity is all imaginative and make-believe. This age makes up its own rules as it goes along. If you play baseball with them they want thirty-seven strikes before they are out. The same youngsters at ten are sticklers for rules.

Work with a ten-year-old on grammar. He calls it "stupid old stuff," and he cannot for the life of him see what difference it makes. That same child at sixteen drives his parents crazy because he corrects every little mistake they make.

Or at ten again, the average girl thinks any boy is a nightmare. Let the girl live six more years: The boy becomes a dreamboat.

As we grow we have needs. We seek certain satisfactions which are the food for our development. At different times in our growth we want different satisfactions. We are always seeking something, but what we seek is tied in to how old we are, how long we have lived, where we are in our development.

Humans do operate on habit. Many of our daily deeds are just mechanical. We do them without thinking, because once there was some pleasure or reward attached to them. But there are tremendous differences between habits and needs.

Habits are added onto the person. They are grafted on as a result of experience. Needs are built into the person. They are incorporated into him because of his humanity.

Habits go on until they are broken. A need disappears when it is satisfied. A habit stops if you hold out on children. A need settles down if you give in to youngsters.

Habits are superficial; they do not touch the main

path of growth. Needs are fundamental; the youngster who has his fill is free to grow.

Self-importance, self-respect, bigness and power: These are not mere habits. These are fundamental human needs. When you in your classroom work to make youngsters feel big you make them glad they are alive today, and you get in some good licks for tomorrow. Your youngsters will grow up to be better parents, better bosses, better workers, better citizens.

"Must You Cater to Children?"

Meeting children's needs sounds to some people like "catering to children." That idea is very offensive. They don't like it in the least. An adult is supposed to be an adult, not someone who gives in to youngsters.

Cater is a strong and strange word, but you can give it a Child Development meaning. Child Development says that children are people. They have feelings. They have ideas of their own. They have preferences. They have leanings—likes and dislikes.

You can put a piece of furniture any place you

like; the furniture does not care. You can drive your car slow or fast, every day or once in a blue moon; it does not make any difference to the car. But you do have to think about people: What will please them? Displease them? What will make them feel better or worse?

You do this with guests in your home. You do not play canasta if your guests are bridge fiends. You do not serve steak if your guest has just lost all of his teeth. You do not turn the television set on if your guests are having a serious conversation. You try to do the decent thing. You try to make people happy. You want to please people, and you are not ashamed to try.

One of the great changes in American life is that we are struggling to be decent to children. We are making an effort to treat them as we would like to be treated. This is a new idea. In many parts of the world children are . . . children. Like sticks. Or lower class. Or second class. It does not matter what you do to them: Do whatever you feel like, whatever is good for you, whatever pops into your head.

This way is the easy way. You don't have to think of the other fellow. He does not count. Whole countries are still run on this basis. Factories, mines, farms, businesses used to be, the world over. But gradually, in America particularly, but elsewhere too, our conscience is being heard: Citizens are people . . . women are people . . . natives are people . . . workers are people. . . .

Our country has been one of the first to take the next step: Children are people. That is a step to feel proud of. We have begun to ask ourselves: "What is a child after?" The question complicates life, but it is a sign of our decency that we have begun to ask it.

You have every right to feel good about what you do. You will make mistakes sometimes, but gearing your efforts to the needs and interests of children is worthwhile. No matter how you keep score you can know in your heart: Yours is a democratic, a reasonable effort. Your children will increasingly feel right; each day as they live will be more satisfying. You can hardly ask for more than that.

5

Your Youngsters Can Climb the Highest Peaks

*C*hild Development's most cheering fact is that the decent way of working with children is also the efficient way! Decency pays off. When you are friendly, when you help children to feel able and growing, you get the best out of youngsters. You make it easy for them to mature. You provide stabilizers and strengtheners for their growth. You make more sure that the time will come when youngsters are sturdy, sound, healthy citizens. You deserve to feel right; children will feel right; our

140

nation, with its great stake in children, can feel both safe and proud. Youngsters whose basic needs are met are free to learn at their best, free to grow to their peaks.

What is that best? How high are those peaks? No one knows for sure, but this much is completely certain: *As the human grows he heads more and more in the direction that makes good human living possible.*

Children grow and develop, but not hit or miss. They grow, but not helter-skelter, or by guess and by chance. They grow, but not all higgledy-piggledy and any-which-way. Growth has a direction. Growth leads the child toward goals each of us treasures. Growth means increasing usefulness to others and increasing satisfaction to one's self.

The infant screams. Growth does not mean more screams and louder ones as time goes on. Growth heads the child toward talking. On the way he will bite when he is unhappy. He will kick. He will spit. But the child is ever going toward the use of words as his mature means of communication.

The infant makes a fist. Growth does not mean bigger and stronger fists, more cruel and harsh, more hurting. Growth heads the child toward reason. **On the way he will grab and push.** But the child is ever moving toward discussion and the exchange of ideas as his eventual human method.

Intellectually the very young child is a me-firster, the isolationist personified. He knows of nothing but his immediate surroundings. He lives in the here and now, this moment of today only. Soon he will remember a yesterday. He will be able to conceive of a tomorrow.

The infant's rattle slips from his fist. He does not even have a problem. The rattle is gone and out of mind. The three-year-old's ball rolls behind a bush. The child has grown enough to know he has a problem . . . but one he cannot solve. He shakes the bush. He shakes the bush again. He yanks, he tugs, he kicks, he shakes. His intellectual tool kit is big enough for only one approach. If that does not work either tears come or he walks away. It is either: "I can't" or "I don't want the old ball anyhow."

But this brain will grow. Each year it will see more problems to solve. It will notice details and relationships that once were lost in dimness. It will dream of possibilities for betterment that once could not be brought to mind. And the brain's whole range of attack will become infinitely more varied.

The infant is not even aware of himself. He looks, but he does not know that he is he. One day he will realize that he is *someone* and for a while his whole world will be centered in himself. /*His* ideas, *his* wishes, *his* wants, *his* train of thought—these are all that will count. But the healthy, growing person does not stop here. This baby eventually will be capable of the self-sacrifice of a parent, of the self-denial of a patriot.

A two-year-old must play alone. He can be near others, in a peaceful state of coexistence. He can watch others, in a state of watchful waiting. But this child is headed toward a brotherhood of man. Even the three-year-old has a friend. The Five has many friends. The Nine has firm friends. The Fifteen has a close friend. The twenty-five-year-old has a family. And the final growth of social interest, of concern, of fellow-feeling need not stop there.

Emotionally the baby can respond solely to his own personal wants. Feed him, and he is happy. Sleep him, and he is happy. Change him, and he is happy. He knows two kinds of feelings, comfort and discomfort, black or white.

Soon he will be capable of more than the simple body-full flood of the temper tantrum. He will know irritation, vexation, worry, and dismay. He will grow from mere interest into sympathy, and the time will come when he can feel grief.

In the beginning pleasure centers in the infant's lips, his belly, his buttocks. He will grow until he is able to share in a friend's success. He will grow until he can become elated at the victory of an idea. He will grow until he can be moved by the well-being or distress of souls he has never met, in lands he has never seen, under conditions he has never experienced.

A direction indicator is set. An "automatic pilot" is at the controls. And a strong motor—call it growth—is purring smoothly inside each child. The motor powers a magnificent brain, an amazing body, a full, fine range of feeling. Your good teaching greases this motor and keeps it in shape. When your youngsters like you, when they like their work, when they like themselves, the motor hums and spins.

Your job is not an easy one. You never have all the tools you need. You have far too many motors to service. There are many pages missing from the "manual of instructions," and even when the directions are there in print, they are never completely clear. Nor are any of us old hands at this way of living with children; we are all puzzling and groping for the appropriate things to do. Hecklers are on the sidelines, looking for perfection, all too willing to remind you that you are feeling your way along.

Once you truly regard the child as a human—caring, seeking, preferring, needing—you have to work. You have to think, to use your judgment and your sensitivity. But the motor is running, and the course is charted. How far will the human go? How fast? For how long? With your good treatment new records are possible: of reason and decency, of kindliness, of caring. The task is well worth the effort of your hands, the time of your head, and the searching of your heart.